THE POCKET IDIOT'S GUIDE™ TO

Betting on Horses

by Sharon B. Smith

alpha books

A Division of Macmillan General Reference
A Pearson Education Macmillan Company
1633 Broadway, New York, NY 10019

The POCKET IDIOT'S GUIDE TO & design are trademarks of Macmillan, Inc.

Macmillan General Reference books may be purchased for business or sales promotional use. For information please write: Special Markets Department, Macmillan Publishing USA, 1633 Broadway, New York, NY 10019.

International Standard Book Number: 1-58245-109-5
Library of Congress Catalog Card Number: A catalogue record is available from the Library of Congress.

01 00 99   4 3 2 1

Interpretation of the printing code: The rightmost number of the first series of numbers is the year of the book's printing; the rightmost number of the second series of numbers is the number of the book's printing. For example, a printing code of 99-1 shows that the first printing occurred in 1999.

Printed in the United States of America

Note: This publication contains the opinions and ideas of its author. It is intended to provide helpful and informative material on the subject matter covered. It is sold with the understanding that the author and publisher are not engaged in rendering professional services in the book. If the reader requires personal assistance or advice, a competent professional should be consulted.

Charts courtesy of the New York Racing Association, the United States Trotting Association, and Equibase.

Alpha Development Team

Publisher
Kathy Nebenhaus

Editorial Director
Gary M. Krebs

Managing Editor
Bob Shuman

Marketing Brand Manager
Felice Primeau

Acquisitions Editor
Jessica Faust

Development Editors
Phil Kitchel
Amy Zavatto

Assistant Editor
Georgette Blau

Production Team

Development Editors
Dominique DeVito
Madelyn Larsen

Production Editor
Carol Sheehan

Copy Editor
Heather Stith

Cover Designer
Mike Freeland

Photo Editor
Richard H. Fox

Cartoonist
Kevin Spear

Designer
Glenn Larsen

Indexer
Nadia Ibrahim

Production Team
Wil Cruz, Teri Edwards, Marie Kristine Parial-Leonardo,
Donna Martin, Sean Monkhouse

Contents

Introduction

There are two major and two slightly minor forms of modern American horse racing. The two big ones are Thoroughbred and Standardbred (or harness) racing. Quarter Horse racing comes next, followed by steeple-chasing. Most books you see take one of two approaches: They cover only one and ignore the rest altogether, or they concentrate on one and ghettoize the others into separate and much smaller sections. That's never been a good idea, and it's an even worse one today.

In this book, I treat horse racing as horse racing. It's true there are differences between the sports, and these are noted as we go along, but most of the information here applies to each of the racing sports. Instead of separating the sports, we separate the facts you need into categories you can understand.

First, we look at the horses. No matter what some books might claim, nobody can talk to horses. Let me revise that. You can talk to them, but none have ever responded. Their language skills are limited. You can, however, observe them, analyze them, and even come to understand them. That's the first level of understanding you need if you hope to win at the racetrack.

Then, we'll move on to people, namely jockeys and drivers. You must know their roles, intentions, skills and experience in order to succeed at the betting windows.

The races themselves come next. The tracks and the competitions held on them form a fourth partner in the relationship of horse, horseman, and bettor, one that's silent in the normal sense but whose characteristics make the difference between winning and losing.

Finally, we examine the process of betting on horse racing. Some people are perfectly happy just going to the racetrack or watching races on television, getting sufficient satisfaction from the beauty and excitement of the sport. But more of us like to be part of the spectacle. We love to predict who's likely to run well and guess who doesn't have a chance. We love to cheer when there's money and not just honor on the line. Most of all, we love to win, whether it's two dollars or a lot more than that. This book will help you become an informed observer of racing, whether you watch for the sport and spectacle or whether you're hoping to earn back the price of your admission to the track.

Extras

These boxes give you ideas, tips, warnings, and interesting information that will help you understand what's going on at the racetrack.

From the Horse's Mouth

If you learn the words in this box, you'll not only sound like you know your way around the racetrack, you'll understand tips, information, and facts that you overhear while watching the races.

Bad Bet

Some horses don't deserve your money, and this box will help you to find and avoid them.

Inside Track

The useful tips in these boxes will help you identify the possible winners before you lay out your money.

Chapter 1

Man, Meet Horse

Man first met horse at the end of a spear point. It was a momentous meeting for each species. In the horse's original home, North America, the meeting and subsequent overhunting by man contributed to the animal's eventual extinction on his native continent. In Asia, the refuge of the surviving horses, the encounter led to a relationship much more profitable for both.

There's no record of the world's first horse race—there weren't any chart callers in attendance—but it probably happened about 5,000 years ago somewhere in central Asia. We don't even know for sure whether the first racehorses were ridden or driven. Most likely, they were driven, because most horses then were much smaller than they are today.

The first recorded horse races occurred somewhere in Greece before 1200 B.C. By the time of the Trojan Wars, racing was a well-established sport. Legend has it that the wars began over the kidnapping of the beautiful Helen of Troy, but Homer's *Iliad* gives the impression that the kidnapping of a couple of equally beautiful Trojan racing stallions helped keep it going. The Greek warrior Diomedes won an important chariot race, the first race to go down in the record books, with the stolen pair. Homer didn't mention the odds.

Four hundred years later, the very first Olympic Games featured mule chariot racing, followed a few Olympiads later by horse racing, both chariot and ridden. Here's where we first hear about race fixing, in which the nefarious tool was fermented mead. History neglects to say whether the mead was supposed to make the horses run faster or slower, but it does tell us that fixers were punished by having to build a statue to Zeus on Mount Olympus.

The Foundations of Modern Racing

Henry VIII loved racing so much that he required his dukes to maintain racing stables. His daughter Elizabeth also enjoyed racing, but it was first called the Sport of Kings during the reign of her heir, James I.

The horse-loving King James did two important things (beyond sponsoring a new version of the Bible, of course). First, he built a royal residence in the quiet country town of Newmarket and, by either great insight or sheer luck, drew attention and horses to one of the three or four best regions in the world to breed and raise horses.

James I also encouraged British breeders to lighten up. He believed that the heavy English horses weren't as fast as they might be, and he himself imported a couple of Arab stallions for crossbreeding.

The Puritan rebel Oliver Cromwell did his best to suppress horse racing during his brief dictatorship during the 17th century, but the restoration of Charles II to the throne saw the restoration of racing, too. With Charles II, modern horse racing was off and running.

Inside Track

In modern racing, two-year-olds compete within their own age group. Three-year-olds also stay in their division until summer, and then most go into all-age races. The older horse, unless clearly geriatric, is usually the best bet.

Every one of today's racehorses, whether Thoroughbred, Standardbred, Quarter Horse, or steeplechaser, descends in one line or another from one of three Middle Eastern stallions imported into England following the reign of Charles II. These three, the Byerly Turk, the Darley Arabian, and the Godolphin Arabian, were the founding fathers of the Thoroughbred breed. The Thoroughbred, in turn, was the ancestor of all other racing breeds.

The Founding Fathers of American Racing

Diomed, the first Epsom Derby winner, was a modest success in England during the first few years of his breeding career. By 1798, he was an elderly 21 and unwanted, except by American breeders. For 10 years, Diomed repaid the country that gave him a second chance by fathering a dynasty of fine racehorses and excellent breeding animals. His great-grandson Lexington, the most influential Thoroughbred of the 19th century, appears in the pedigrees of almost every winner of *stakes races* in the world today.

From the Horse's Mouth

The **stakes race** represents the highest level of horse racing. Horses are either invited by the track or staked to the race by a fee paid by their owners. The fees are added to the purse, so stakes are sometimes called added money races.

In 1756, a little English Thoroughbred named Janus arrived in Virginia to be bred to local mares with the hopes of producing offspring capable of winning the four-mile races then popular. But Janus persisted in producing stocky little short-distance horses like himself, becoming the founding father of the entire Quarter Horse breed.

In 1788, a gray stallion named Messenger arrived from England, disembarking in Philadelphia. He had been a modestly successful racehorse in England but wasn't considered good enough to be used at stud in his native country. Messenger was plenty good enough for America, becoming the maternal grandsire of the continent's first racing star, American Eclipse, as well as the paternal grandsire of Rysdyk's Hambletonian, the founder of the Standardbred breed.

And Then They Evolved

Although their ancestry is similar, the three modern racing breeds began to diverge dramatically during the mid–19th century, leading to the racehorses and the racing sports we know today. Racing people like to say that God made the horse, but man made the Thoroughbred. This statement is true and quite a compliment to man.

The Thoroughbred

Any modern Thoroughbred is a remarkably well-documented creature. Even the most determined human genealogist isn't likely to know the names of every one of his ancestors, plus all their brothers, sisters, aunts, uncles, children, and in-laws for more than 22 generations. English Thoroughbreds do (or their human owners do). American Thoroughbreds may have a few unidentified black sheep in their pedigrees, although none for at least a hundred years.

But if you go back 23 generations or so, you might have a little trouble figuring out just who contributed genes to the Thoroughbred. We know that the Arab-type horses imported into England 300 years ago supplied fine thin legs, light body structure, and elegant heads. We suspect that English horses of previous centuries offered size, muscle, and heavy bone. There were probably even a few pony ancestors.

What this genetic mix means is that today's Thoroughbred can vary in appearance and physique. Some variations matter when you bet on a horse, and some don't.

Color

Color is undoubtedly the least important physical characteristic of a racehorse, at least in terms of racing ability.
Color helps you spot your choice on the far side of the
racetrack, and sometimes it does a little more than that.

From the Horse's Mouth

A **bay** horse is red or brown with a black mane and tail; a
chestnut is reddish; a **gray** or **roan** has white hairs intermixed with a darker color. A **dark bay** or **brown** horse
looks black to anyone with normal eyesight.

No color is automatically superior to any other color in
terms of speed or stamina, although breeders, owners,
trainers, and bettors each have their prejudices. However,
there's one case where it might matter (just a little, to be
sure).

A horse that looks like a parent in build and color is some-
what more likely to run like that parent, and color is a
factor to consider if you don't know much else about the
horse. Make it part of your decision if you're thinking
about betting on an unraced two-year-old or you're trying
to pick the Kentucky Derby winner out of a field of
horses, none of whom has ever been asked to run a mile
and a quarter.

Bad Bet

Don't assume too much because of the tendency of horses who look like a parent to run like them. Big red Secretariat's best racing offspring was little gray Lady's Secret.

White on the lower leg also has no effect at all on racing ability, but some experts think that a white leg combined with a white hoof is a warning sign. White hoof walls are softer than dark ones, sometimes making nails more likely to pull loose.

Height

Watch any field of Thoroughbreds heading to the starting gate, and you'll see a group of horses fairly similar in height and weight. In some circumstances, being shorter or taller than average can be an advantage for a horse. In other cases, it can be limiting.

From the Horse's Mouth

A **hand** is 4 inches. Horse height is measured from the ground to the high point of the **withers,** the top of the shoulder just in front of the saddle. A horse who's 16.3 hands, for example, is 16 hands 3 inches or 67 inches tall at the withers.

Consider these points before betting on an unusually tall horse:

➤ If the race is very short (under 6 *furlongs*), a tall horse may have trouble. Tall horses usually don't break out of the starting gate as quickly as smaller ones, and a short race gives him little time to make up for a poor start.

From the Horse's Mouth

A **furlong** is ⅛ of a mile. It's the primary unit of race measurement in North America and in Britain, although much of the rest of the racing world uses kilometers and meters.

➤ A racetrack with sharp turns can be difficult for a tall horse. Watch out if your tall bet is running on a racetrack less than a mile around or one with a flattened oval shape.

➤ A tall horse usually has a long stride and can do well on a track that features wide, sweeping turns and a long stretch.

➤ Tall horses usually excel in steeplechasing or any other racing over fences. They dominate in events with wide or high fences.

Short horses enjoy an advantage in the following situations:

➤ Short horses have greater agility out of the starting gate, which gives them a big advantage in short races. The shorter the race, the more likely it is that a short horse will win.

➤ A race in which the first turn comes soon after the start is made to order for short horses, who can get themselves into full stride quickly.

➤ Surprisingly, short horses often have greater stamina than tall ones, even though you might assume that their shorter strides would make them work harder during a race. The greater stamina is probably because their comparatively light body structure means less weight to haul around the racetrack. A short, stocky horse loses this advantage.

Thoroughbred Conformation

Body shape and structure affect both speed and stamina. We'll look at some of the characteristics that differentiate a slow horse from a fast one and a horse that can sail through a mile and a half from one who's gasping for breath after 6 furlongs.

Hindquarters

The horse's hindquarters make up his power train. They're the best indicator of speed potential.

➤ Horses with wide hindquarters usually have more pure speed than horses with narrow ones. Their wider centers of balance also make them quicker and more secure out of the starting gate.

➤ Horses with narrower hindquarters and the resulting lower body weight are more likely to excel at a distance, and a less-than-snappy start won't matter if there's a long race ahead.

Head

The other end of the horse can also indicate speediness. The head itself doesn't have much to do with it, no matter how some people—including expert horsemen—are convinced that a horse with piggy little eyes or clown-like floppy ears can't possibly run fast. They can, and they often do.

Bad Bet

Watch out for the horse whose head carriage changes dramatically once the gate opens. The high-headed sprinter type becomes a low-headed distance runner. Note it for next time.

How the horse carries his head does matter. A horse with a high head may look proud and impressive, but he probably won't be able to keep his speed up much beyond a sprint distance. The short breaths and short strides that result from the high head carriage will see to that.

Chest

Drop your gaze a couple of feet to the horse's chest. From the front, you want to see enough width of chest and rib cage to accommodate lung expansion. Lung capacity is more important for horses expected to run a distance, so a narrow-chested horse—while not desirable—may be a reasonable bet in a short race.

From a side view, look for shoulder depth and slope rather than size. A long, sloping shoulder means a long stride—a necessity for any horse expected to run farther than six or 7 furlongs.

If you have a good eye, you may be able to predict stride length at the gallop by watching the horse in the *walking ring* or the *post parade*. At the walk, a horse that sets his back feet down in front of where his forefeet had been will probably have a long stride at the faster gaits, too.

From the Horse's Mouth

The horses amble around the **walking ring** after being saddled and before moving onto the track, where they begin walking in front of the stands in the **post parade**.

Back

Judge the horse's back length by estimating the amount of back visible between the end of the saddle and the point at which the hindquarters start to rise up. The back, whether short or long, has little relationship to speed, but it can play a role in racing success:

➤ Short backs are usually stronger and less subject to injury than long ones. A short-backed horse can usually carry more weight without discomfort, making him a natural for races in which a lot of weight is assigned.

➤ But those races—especially steeplechases or other races over fences—also come with taller riders. Short-backed horses sometimes don't have space for tall riders, making them poor candidates for victory. What's more, short-backed horses often can't manage a decent arc over jumps and lose precious ground when racing over fences. The key in steeplechases is this: the horse's back should be short enough to stay healthy, but long enough to accommodate the rider.

➤ In flat races, particularly in cases where the horse is expected to carry weight, shorter is better than longer.

Other Characteristics

Here's a sampler of other physical characteristics that contribute to speed and racing ability:

➤ **Thin is best for fashion models, chimney sweeps, and winning racehorses.** A horse whose bone structure is hidden under a layer of fat isn't in good enough condition to win.

➤ **Feet count.** Ideally, all racehorses should have hooves proportional in size to their bodies. Some very fast horses have very small feet, but distance horses, turf runners, and good performers in the mud almost never do. Big feet are good in mud and on turf; small feet are good in dirt-track sprints.

➤ **Noses matter, too.** Tiny nostrils make it difficult for a horse to take in air; too-large ones can mean a breathing problem. Both faults are more noticeable over a longer distance.

The Standardbred

Standardbreds, although they have more Thoroughbred blood than anything else, wouldn't be racing at the trot and pace while pulling a vehicle if there weren't other genetic contributors as well. The most important was the now-extinct Trotter, an old English coaching breed that was never used for competitive racing. The Norfolk Trotter had a healthy dose of Thoroughbred blood himself, but he had heavier bone and more muscle. He also had physical characteristics that enabled him to trot smoothly and very rapidly.

American farmers and others interested in moving their goods and themselves as quickly as possible naturally wanted Norfolk Trotter blood, and they imported plenty of it. Some of it found its way into the Morgan breed, and Morgans—as well as more direct Norfolk Trotter descendants—combined with the Thoroughbred during the mid–19th century to provide most of the genes to the Standardbred pool.

What Makes a Standardbred?

Standardbreds, trotters or pacers, have a lot in common with each other in spite of their different gaits. Let's look first at similarities.

Size

Most Standardbreds, regardless of gait, tend to be shorter than Thoroughbreds but slightly heavier in body structure. Most successful Standardbreds are between 15 and 16 hands tall.

Color

Both trotters and pacers are usually bay, occasionally chestnut or brown, rarely gray, and never paint or pinto. Most have little white on their legs or faces. Some of this uniformity of color occurs because racing people prefer it.

Temperament

Most Standardbreds are good-natured and easy to manage, partially because they get a lot of handling very early in their lives. In addition, the process of hooking a horse to a vehicle requires an animal that cooperates. Difficult horses have to be remarkably good to get a chance to race. They have to be even better to be bred because nobody in harness racing wants to perpetuate bad temper genes.

The Differences Between Trotters and Pacers

There are important differences between the two kinds of harness horses, besides the obvious one of their racing gaits. The pace has distinct physical requirements, and the two gaits are different enough that an astute observer can tell whether a horse is a *trotter* or *pacer* merely by watching him graze in the field.

From the Horse's Mouth

The **trot,** a gait midway between the walk and the run, features legs on opposite corners moving together. It's the gait of most four-legged animals. The **pace,** performed by camels, a few breeds of dogs, and pacing horses, features legs on the same side moving backward and forward at the same time. Pacers are sometimes called amblers or side-wheelers.

Trotting Horse Characteristics

Although less than 20 percent of today's harness races in North America feature trotters, some of the most prestigious ones do, including the Hambletonian, the Dexter Cup, and the Kentucky Futurity. There are also plenty of lower-level trotting races, particularly for young horses.

Here are some of the physical characteristics to look for in your trotting candidate:

➤ Among trotters, there may be no great advantage to height, but body length does matter. The nature of the gait makes interference between front legs and hind legs possible as the horse reaches for more speed. Although there are plenty of exceptions, most good trotters are at least as many inches long in the body as they are in height at the withers.

➤ A fast trot is best performed by a horse with large hindquarters because the gait is based on rear propulsion. You'll often see good trotters whose hindquarters are higher than their withers as viewed from the side. This horse is referred to as being built *downhill*. For a trotter, going downhill doesn't mean he's no longer the horse he used to be. It's a description of good trotter shape.

➤ People used to think that trotters needed a lot of bend in their rear legs to be fast, but this was probably because the great Hambletonian transmitted this characteristic to his offspring. Some horses trot well with straight hind legs; some trot well with a dramatic bend in the legs. Don't worry about it.

➤ Do worry, though, if you're eyeing a trotter whose hind legs bow inward at the hocks as viewed from behind. These *cow hocks* (so named because every cow you meet, fast or slow, has them) cause a horse's rear hooves to rotate inward at a fast trot, often striking the opposite front foot. This interference makes a smooth, fast trot almost impossible for the horse to maintain.

From the Horse's Mouth

The **hock** is the rear leg equivalent of the knee.

Pacing Horse Characteristics

No matter what day you go to the harness races in North America, even Hambletonian Day at the Meadowlands, you'll see more races for pacers than trotters. So put most of your effort into identifying good pacing body type.

➤ Good pacers tend to be blockier than trotters, with comparatively short bodies and wide chests. Narrow-chested pacers can move as fast as others, but they often *crossfire,* causing injury to themselves or causing them to be slowed by the equipment that prevents the injury.

From the Horse's Mouth

Crossfiring occurs when one hoof strikes the hoof or leg on the other side. The left hind foot, for example, raps the right front foot.

➤ The pace is powered almost as much from the shoulders as the hindquarters, so you'll see good pacers with narrower hindquarters and more pronounced shoulders than trotters. Pacers with withers higher than their hindquarters are said to be built *uphill.* For a pacer, it can be an advantage.

➤ Cow hocks present few problems to pacers, unless they're so severe that the horse can't keep his balance.

Quarter Racing Horses

Note the name of the section. Although they're members of the same breed, Quarter Horses and Quarter Racing Horses are not exactly the same thing. Nowadays, Quarter Horses who race are more like Thoroughbreds than they are like roping horses, cutting horses, steer-wrestling horses, or any other members of their own breed. Once you've learned to pick a Thoroughbred who should perform well in short races, you can pick a Quarter Horse with the potential to win in his own sport.

There are two reasons for all those Thoroughbred genes. The American Quarter Horse Association, the breed's registry, wasn't established until 1940. Before then, owners of quick little western horses who wanted more size and elegance bred their animals to Thoroughbreds. After 1940, the new registration rules conveniently permitted these habits to continue.

Each decade that passes sees the Quarter Horses used in racing become more and more Thoroughbred. But there are still a few differences between the breeds, although the differences may be just a matter of degree. Quarter Horse races are shorter than normal Thoroughbred sprints; the standard distances range from 220 to 400 yards. So a Quarter Horse with the potential to win should be like his sprinting Thoroughbred cousin, only more so.

There are a few special characteristics to look for in a Quarter Racing Horse.

Size

For every horse generation that passes, the Quarter Racing Horse becomes taller. He's still shorter than the average Thoroughbred (14.3 to 15.3 hands) because height is not an advantage and breeders aren't attracted to tall stallions even if they want more Thoroughbred blood.

Too much height is a disadvantage because longer legs and a lengthier stride go along with it. The long-striding horse can rarely get himself into top gear before a Quarter Horse race is over.

Quarter Horses are likely to be heavier than Thoroughbreds of similar size because they need solid bone to take the stress of sudden acceleration. They also need plenty of heavy muscle, particularly in the rear end.

Hindquarters

A Quarter Horse without substantial hindquarters isn't going to have the power to get out of the starting gate quickly and will fail at racing. There are almost no exceptions to this rule. No rear, no horse.

Body Length

Quarter Racing Horses should be short-bodied and stocky, at least compared to Thoroughbreds, because this body type can survive the pounding of the short, all-out stride necessary in a race of a quarter mile or less. It's an inflexible body type, but that doesn't matter. Standard-length Quarter Horse races are run on the straightaway, and turns play no role at all.

Head and Neck

The Quarter Racing Horse needs to carry his head and neck higher than the Thoroughbred because he's going to

have to be able to break out of the starting gate completely alert. Some good horses carry their heads low at
the walk, and then bring them up at the gallop. Others
never get them up and always lose ground at the start.

Chapter 2

The Race Goes to the Swift...

In This Chapter

➤ The different kinds of speed

➤ Workouts and speed

➤ What's fast and what's not

In all the racing breeds, success at two and three years of age is the best indicator of natural speed. By following this guideline, you'll eliminate a few fast horses that were slow to mature, but you'll also eliminate most of the winners who succeeded because of qualities other than speed.

Stallions who raced well themselves while young are the most successful in breeding, but those who only raced while young may have had short careers because of problems with health and soundness. These problems are often transmitted to their offspring, but they usually don't affect individual races.

From the Horse's Mouth

The **sire** is the father, the **dam** is the mother, and the **foal** is the baby. Other words to know: A **stallion** is an adult male horse; a **mare** is an adult female.

In Thoroughbred racing, fast horses rarely run equally fast from the starting gate to the finish line. There are variations on the speed theme, some admirable and some undesirable.

Cheap Speed

A horse with the breeding and conformation to run fast may be described as having *cheap speed*. Cheap speed is speed that fades before it should. Possessors of cheap speed dash out of the starting gate or, occasionally, out of a pack of horses while the race is underway, getting themselves to or near the lead. Then they proceed to slow down and lose.

Nobody wants to ride, train, or bet on a horse with cheap speed because the finish line always seems to come too late, no matter how short the race. This means that disappointment is coupled with frustration and annoyance.

Horses who have it are usually thought to have no guts, although they generally have the same problems that plague other losers in every kind of racing:

➤ They hurt, and the pain starts after a short distance of racing.

> ➤ They don't have much talent to begin with.

> ➤ They may not be well-trained.

> ➤ They don't understand what racing really requires.

Most horses with cheap speed also possess a characteristic shared by almost all racehorses, fast, slow, or in-between. They can make one effort, and only one, to run fast during a race.

Early Speed

Horses with early speed break out of the gate quickly, challenge for the lead immediately, and then run as fast as possible as long as possible. Most horses can't run at anything resembling top speed for more than 6 furlongs, but this effort is enough to win the majority of races run in North America. Brilliant early speed is a fine thing to have, provided your ambition isn't to win a Triple Crown race.

Just how long early speed can hold and whether it can last as long as or longer than 6 furlongs depends on a lot of factors other than the horse who possesses it, including track design, racing surface, post position, and the characteristics of the rest of the field.

Late Speed

In order to have any shot at winning, a horse has to be running at the end. Horses who save their one run for late in the race are just as admirable as horses with early speed, but the results of their races are more affected by outside influences. Other horses running faster or slower than expected, bulky fields that give them nowhere to make their runs, accidents in front of them—the late runner can be devastated by all these unforeseen events.

Horses with late speed have been known to make suckers of bettors. A horse who's always running fast and well at the end, making up yardage with every stride and gaining on the leaders as the finish line approaches, convinces a lot of people that he'll win it all next time, provided the race is just a little longer. Sometimes that's true, but some horses never seem to get there, no matter how long the race. Late speed in a long race is not necessarily a formula for success.

Standardbred Speed

Early and late speed exist in harness racing, but they often result more from human strategy than equine preference. All Standardbreds are bred to compete at the standard one-mile distance. Some do have more natural speed, and some do have more stamina, but the variations aren't as pronounced as they are in Thoroughbred racing.

Early speed is most important in races on harness tracks a half-mile in circumference because a horse who doesn't get himself into contention early probably finds it impossible to pass horses on the short straightaways and the four sharp turns. Late speed is required on the one-mile tracks and those 5/8-mile tracks that feature wide, sweeping turns.

Workouts and Speed

In Thoroughbred racing, morning gallops are the workouts that provide information. In Standardbred racing, you'll be looking mostly at qualifying races because harness workouts are usually not conducted in public, and the results are not published. In Quarter Horse racing, horses are worked in the morning, but meaningful workouts are both less frequent and less public than in Thoroughbred racing. If you do hear numbers, you may take them into consideration, particularly with first-time starters at well-organized racetracks.

Bad Bet

Never read anything into the fact that harness horses aren't worked in public. That's the tradition, even among the horses that are stabled at the racetrack.

Although most racehorses come out of their stalls every morning for exercise, not all of these expeditions qualify as workouts. Sometimes, the horses are simply led around the barns; on other days, they're asked to do a slow jog on the track.

Even formal workouts vary. Here are the kinds of workouts you are most likely to read or hear about, along with their commonly accepted definitions:

➤ Breezing (noted by the symbol *b* in lists or charts) means that the horse galloped without serious urging by his rider.

➤ Handily (noted by *h*) means the rider urged the horse for more speed.

➤ Driving (noted by a capital *D*) means the horse was asked for racing speed. This is an uncommon occurrence in workouts.

➤ Other notes you may see: A *g* means the horse worked out of the starting gate. A small *d* means that dogs were up on the track. No, the horse didn't have to dodge yelping canines, but he did have to run a little wide, because barriers were placed on the track to keep the working horses away from the rail. Both a *g* and a *d* means you have to subtract at least half of a second from the horse's time to compare it with other workouts on the same day at the same distance.

From the Horse's Mouth

In harness racing, you'll often hear the word **train** instead of *work* for the serious exercise that includes performing at close to racing speed.

You have to spend time figuring out all these symbols only if the workout was done in public. Most Thoroughbreds train at the racetrack, but some are kept at private training centers. You'll never hear about many of these workouts, except in rumor or gossip.

Some trainers who don't have access to private training tracks hold their public workouts in private by sending their horses out before the sun rises. Some trainers like to send their horses out very early so they get first crack at a pristine track surface; others just don't like the idea of other people assessing their horses' readiness.

In Thoroughbred racing, respectable public workouts are conducted in daylight under the control and direction of racetrack personnel. They're the only kind that provide useful information to the average racegoer, although, as you'll soon see, the quality of the information is occasionally suspect.

Some racing jurisdictions require horses to show up for at least one public timed workout before they are permitted to race. But remember that a horse forced to work for official clockers provides the most suspect information of all. He probably won't be asked for much of an effort by his exercise rider.

The Hand That Holds the Stopwatch

Workout times are only as good as the people who control the stopwatches. Human timers, known at the track as *clockers*, vary in their talents. Some clockers work for race-tracks; others work for the *Daily Racing Form* and other suppliers of racetrack data.

We'll have more later on how to find and read past performance information, but note that a workout line, usually at the bottom of the list of the horse's previous races, will read something like this:

Latest Workout Jul 7 Bel 4f fst 49 2/5 h *3/21*

It means that the horse worked at Belmont Park on July 7, going 4 furlongs on a fast track handily (under urging) in $49^2/_5$ seconds. He was third fastest of 21 horses who worked that distance on July 7.

Another useful source of workout information is in past performance publications, including the *Form,* but it requires that you clip or remember figures that might not be useful for weeks. The *daily workout tabulation* lists all workouts for each day at a given racetrack. They're published with the horses' names in alphabetical order, and they sometimes include interesting tidbits at the bottom that highlight a handful of individual horses.

Tabulations allow you to judge the quality of an individual horse's workout, enabling you to determine exactly how much speed he showed. In comparison, the past performance workout line includes the *bullet* workout symbol as well as the horse's standing for the day, but it doesn't let you judge how the workout compares. Third fastest might just be a fraction faster than 21st fastest, or it might be seconds faster.

From the Horse's Mouth

The **bullet** work is the fastest of the day, symbolized by a big black dot to the left of the horse's name.

To judge speed, you need to know how fast other horses were running on the morning of the workout. You might see a figure that suggests brilliant speed, but the tabulation might tell you that the horse was faster than only 3 of 50 horses who worked that day. The speed was in the racetrack.

What's Fast and What's Not

This is the big question. In general, at a top-level racetrack in New York, California, or Florida during the winter season, you are permitted to be impressed with handy 4-furlong workouts of 47 $^3/_5$ seconds, 5-furlong workouts of 1:00, and 6-furlong workouts of 1:12 $^4/_5$. In the case of two-year-olds, you'll be looking for signs that the horse can run 3 furlongs in less than 36 seconds, either breezing or handily. Those babies have some speed.

Standardbred Works

Workouts are different for Standardbreds, who tend to race much more often than Thoroughbreds. A healthy harness horse, even a top stakes contender, may race once a week during the height of his season. He keeps himself healthy and sharp by racing.

He's likely to train in private once or twice a week in addition to racing, but he won't be asked for real racing speed in those workouts. What's more, you're not going to hear about them. But there is one kind of race training that you can use to assess the speed of the horses you're considering.

In most places, Standardbreds are required to successfully compete in *qualifying races,* also known as *qualifiers,* before they are allowed to race in betting events. Some experienced horses are also required to requalify, but those horses have problems that we'll talk about later.

From the Horse's Mouth

The **purse** is the prize money in a horse race. Almost all tracks pay prize money for the first four places, some pay a small amount to the fifth place finisher.

The results of qualifying races appear in the past-performance charts that you find in racing programs at harness tracks and in handicapping publications such as *Sports Eye.* They're reported the same way as other races except that you'll see a *Q* or a *Qua* next to the information about the race. There are a couple of things to pay attention to when you're trying to find signs of real speed in a qualifying race:

➤ Qualifiers are rarely as fast as betting races because trainers and owners don't want their horses to be worked too hard when there's no money to be won or bets to be cashed.

Bad Bet

Just before each race, some horses are scored, or asked to trot or pace at top speed for a few hundred yards. This exercise is a lung-opener, not a demonstration of speed. Don't bother trying to time it.

➤ Fast quarter times tell you about a horse's pure speed.

➤ Fast final times tell you whether he's ready to win immediately.

Compare the horse's speed in the qualifier to what other horses have been doing on the same racetrack, allowing for the fact that the horse probably will not have been pushed too hard.

Chapter 3

...But Also to the Sound

OOPS!

In This Chapter

➤ Soundness is second only to speed

➤ Where are all these unsound horses coming from?

➤ How to spot the unsound

➤ Medications: what they do for horses and bettors

Unsoundness can change the outcome of races in several ways:

➤ It can turn a fast horse into a slow one. If it hurts to run fast, most horses slow down.

➤ Unsoundness can assure that a horse won't get beyond a sprint distance, even though he's bred to run farther.

➤ It can cause a horse to bear out on turns or in the stretch, losing yardage just when he should be making up ground.

➤ It is the cause, direct or indirect, of almost all breakdowns, in which a horse is injured so badly that he can't finish a race. Worst of all, unsoundness can lead to catastrophic injury, a disastrous accident to one or more legs from which only the most valuable horses are even given a chance to recover.

Where's It All Coming From?

The first and most significant barrier to soundness in the racehorse is the fact that the sport is physically stressful. The galloping horse uses a four-beat gait. This means that at the various points of the stride, the horse's entire weight is carried on each leg individually. That's half a ton or more of body weight balanced on a single thin leg. The trot and pace are two-beat gaits, with two legs carrying all the weight alternately, but that's still a quarter ton per leg.

Add to that one of the basic laws of physics ($F = M \times A$; *force* equals *mass* times *acceleration*), and you get an extraordinary amount of force exerted on a delicate structure of bone and soft tissue. Breeders could create horses that reduce the mass aspect of the equation by breeding lighter horses, but there remains the belief that bigger horses are faster. It's probably wrong, but it's ingrained.

The Racetrack

The racetrack, the playing field of the sport, may also contribute to unsoundness. In Thoroughbred racing, horses go around one to four turns, depending on the length of the race and the size of the track. In harness racing, they complete two, three, or four turns in a standard-length race, again depending on the track. Quarter Horses are lucky enough to face no turns, unless they're entered in the rare half-mile races.

Inside Track

Steeplechasing is a separate case. Less force is involved in the galloping because the horses are asked for slower speeds and less acceleration. But there's great force exerted on the forelegs as the horse comes down from the jump. Unsound horses can't race over fences, although sometimes they're trained to steeplechase by people who don't know what else to do with them. Beware of first-time starters over fences.

Left to their own devices, horses slow down when they need to gallop or trot around turns in order to take pressure off joints and bones being asked to bend unnaturally. Following that famous law of physics, they reduce force by reducing acceleration. In racing, horses may be allowed to take it easy at the first turn but rarely at the final one because the finish line is just around the corner. The stress on the bones and joints reaches a dangerous level around turns.

The racing surface also contributes to unsoundness. Hard surfaces jar bones and joints more than soft ones, but soft surfaces can cause tendons and ligaments to stretch and pull.

The Horses

Even though soundness and racing success go hand-in-hand, soundness and speed often do not. Breeders, in an effort to get more and more speed in their product, contribute to soundness problems by perpetuating characteristics that make horses unsound. A brilliantly fast horse will get a chance to be bred—provided he lives long enough—even though he himself was chronically unsound.

Sometimes this strategy works well for breeders, owners, and the sport itself. Several of the greatest Thoroughbred stallions of the past 50 years, including Raise a Native, Mr. Prospector, and Danzig, were fast but unsound racehorses. At stud, they transmitted their speed and more soundness than they enjoyed themselves. Others are not so lucky.

Problems You Can See

Some unsoundness remains the secret of the trainer until the day the horse slows down and pulls up limping after the finish line or until he breaks down during the race. Everybody suspects unsoundness after they see a horse euthanized on the racetrack.

But you can see or assume some potential problems in advance. They join the other factors you consider as you decide how to place your bets.

Bucked Shins

Bucked shins are minor injuries to the foreleg, consisting either of microfractures along the front of the *cannon bone* or simpler inflammation of the tissue covering the bone.

They are common in Thoroughbreds and Quarter Horses but rare in Standardbreds. They're caused by placing force on bone not quite ready to withstand it. The Standardbred's gait limits the force enough to protect him.

From the Horse's Mouth

The **cannon bone** is what we call the shinbone in humans; it's the long bone in the front of the leg that runs between the knee and the ankle.

Bucked shins cause pain and swelling along the front of the leg, and most horses slow down because of them. A horse may not limp if both shins are equally sore. Bucked shins happen once in a horse's lifetime and can cause a good horse to lose unexpectedly or an average one to run even worse.

Tendon Injuries

All the racing breeds suffer tendon injuries, many of which you won't be able to see as the horse goes to the post. Most tendon injuries result from too much pull on the tendons at the back of the legs, although some can be caused by a blow.

You can't see minor tendon pulls, but you certainly can see bowed tendons. Bows are a sign of past, present, and future problems for a racehorse. In Thoroughbreds and Quarter Horses, look at the front legs. In the harness horse, bows can appear in front and hind legs equally.

A classic bowed tendon looks like a thickening that runs the length of the back of the lower leg. Other kinds of bows look like big bumps on the back of the cannon bone, either just below the knee, in the middle of the leg, or just above the ankle.

From the Horse's Mouth

The **pastern** is the bone that connects the ankle with the hoof.

Horses can race again after suffering a bowed tendon, but they will almost certainly not race at their previous level. If you see a horse who used to be a major track stakes horse running in low-level events at a small track, take a look at his legs. They may show you why he's a risky bet even against much lower quality horses.

Bad Hocks

The hock, the rear leg equivalent of the knee, is the site of several soundness problems, especially for Standardbreds. You'll often hear any kind of hock pain or injury referred to as *bone spavin,* although there are nonspavin hock problems, most much less serious, that affect racehorses.

Early bone spavin, a form of arthritis, shows up as slight lameness only when the horse is cold. After he warms up, he seems just fine. You'll often see horses going to the post who seem very stiff in their hind legs, but they may do very well and be fine for a bet once the gate opens.

Curbed hocks also need a close look. A *curb* is a slight
thickening of a ligament that connects the hock to the
back of the rear cannon bone. (A curb usually creates a
much smaller bump than a bow.) A *cap* is a bump on the
back of the hock.

Equipment That Shouts Unsoundness

Indications of unsoundness can also be applied to the
horse along with the saddle or harness. Some you can see.
Others are not so visible, and racetracks help you with
these by posting, either on a chalkboard or on the tote
board, information about special equipment. Some tracks
don't post equipment information but do announce it
over the loudspeaker system. This information is important, so pay attention to the announcements.

Bandages

This equipment you can see. Here's the rule in Thoroughbred and Quarter Horse racing: Bandages on the rear legs
may or may not mean soundness problems, but bandages
on the front legs almost always do.

The rear bandages that you don't have to worry about at
all are those that cover the fetlock (rear ankle joint) and
continue a few inches up the cannon bone. These small,
light bandages are called *run-downs* and serve to protect
the skin of the fetlock from irritation from the racetrack
that occurs as the hind feet dig into the surface. At tracks
with deep surfaces, all the horses going to the post may be
wearing run-downs.

Bandages that continue up the rear cannon bone may
be there to give support to the ligaments and tendons
surrounding that bone. If so, somebody (such as the
trainer) has some serious doubts about the horse's
soundness.

Bar Shoes

Most Thoroughbred and Quarter Horse tracks post or announce information about *bar shoes*. These shoes are used to give extra protection to sore hoofs by spreading the concussion over a larger surface. Bar shoes, although they allow some horses to race when they otherwise couldn't, can be dangerous: to you, if he races away with your money because he's still too uncomfortable to win, and to him because one sore foot may cause him to put extra weight on his good feet. The excess stress on one leg causes many catastrophic breakdowns.

From the Horse's Mouth

A **bar shoe** looks like a regular horseshoe except there's an extra segment of steel or aluminum connecting the two ends.

Standardbred Equipment

Harness trainers tend to employ so much equipment to make their horses trot or pace better and faster that it's much more difficult to try to figure out which items mean unsoundness and which are merely experiments. The racing trot and pace are unnaturally extended, and even well-conformed horses can occasionally interfere with themselves, with rear feet striking forelegs, and vice versa. Harness horses often carry an entire *tack* shop's worth of boots, cups, and bandages designed to prevent themselves from cutting or bruising their own bodies.

From the Horse's Mouth

Tack is the equipment used on a horse for riding or driving. Driving equipment is also called rigging.

All this equipment does not necessarily mean the horse is unsound. He may merely have a creative trainer.

The Vet Check

All licensed racetracks have a veterinarian who checks horses before they race. The vets have the authority to order a horse *scratched* if they feel his condition makes racing unsafe for his rider, himself, or other horses. The vets may all be skilled enough to detect an unsound horse, but they vary tremendously in their inclination to order scratches. It's probably because of the policy of their racetracks rather than any preference of their own. At lower-level racetracks that offer small purses, most horses have questionable soundness, and only one with a very severe problem is going to be ordered scratched.

From the Horse's Mouth

A **scratch** is the withdrawal of a horse from a race after he has been announced as an entry.

At a good track, every horse is checked by the vet the morning he's scheduled to be raced. His legs are felt, he is walked in front of the vet, and he may have his temperature and heart checked. Later, he is observed as he warms up, and he's given a visual check as he approaches the starting gate. The vet can order him scratched at any point in the process.

The gate scratch often infuriates bettors, because their bets are automatically transferred to the starting favorite—who usually features much lower odds. Don't be annoyed if it happens to you. A horse who's so unsound that the vet scratches him at the gate is not going to win anything anyway.

The Three Categories of Medication

Drugs used on racehorses can be grouped into three general categories, although the same drug can fit into all three, depending on the circumstances and the intentions of the person who administers it.

➤ Some are intended to cure ailments or alleviate pain. They are believed to have no effect on performance and are permitted as race-day medications, although the quantity the horse may receive is regulated in most states.

➤ Others are therapeutic, but they have side effects that could alter the outcome of races. These are likely to be used for horses in training, but they are not permitted, except in trace amounts, in horses when they race.

➤ Others have no legitimate use in horses other than to alter race results and are illegal if they're detected in any horse scheduled to race. A few of these are illegal whether the horse is scheduled to race or not. Post-race tests, for example, occasionally turn up positive for cocaine. The horse isn't arrested, but he's disqualified, and his people are investigated.

Scientists, horsemen, and bettors are constantly adjusting and readjusting their ideas about which side effects exist and which don't, and which matter to the outcome of a race. Racing authorities also adjust their ideas, although rarely as quickly as the other interested parties.

Most important to racing are the medications known as the Big Two. They are phenylbutazone and furosemide, better known by their most widely distributed brand names, *Butazolodin* and *Lasix*. These medications are permitted in most of North America, usually in controlled doses.

The Big Two have been accepted as widely as they are because of the belief that, although they work on horse ailments, they don't really affect the results of a race. That's nonsense on its face. If a horse doesn't run as well without a drug, the presence of the drug clearly has an effect on the race. But the drug issue is a little more complicated than that. Let's look at each of the two drugs, beginning with the first one to become widespread in the racing business.

Bute

Everybody calls it *bute*, even though its proper and generic name is phenylbutazone. This drug is legal for race-day use in all but a handful of states and Canada. Bute has been used in animals and humans since the late 1950s, primarily as a painkiller for those suffering from orthopedic injuries. If you twist your knee playing tennis, you may leave the doctor's office with a prescription for bute.

Bute has been accepted by racing authorities because it has no effect on the central nervous system and doesn't make a horse run faster or slower than his physical structure, training, or mental inclination permits him to do.

Bute, the authorities think, doesn't make a horse run like anyone but himself.

The primary side effect is a risk of stomach ulcers, a condition that doesn't affect the results of individual races either. The bottom line is that bute is usually a safe, effective drug. It's so cheap—only about $10 a dose—that you'll see races where every starter has been given the drug.

Inside Track

Look for the letter *B* to identify a horse who's been given bute. It will be next to his name in the program or in the past performance charts.

A horse not on bute is very likely to be sound, and you can give him a point or two for that. This is especially important if the horse comes from the barn of a good trainer. You can be moderately confident that the horse is ready to race to the level of his talent, to finish the race on four legs, and to give you a run for your money.

Lasix

The second of the Big Two is called Lasix, even though its generic name is furosemide. It is more controversial and more uniformly permitted than bute.

Lasix debuted on the pharmaceutical stage in the late 1960s as a diuretic for humans. It increases the volume of urine produced by the kidneys, reduces blood pressure, and causes excess fluid in the tissues to decrease. As with most successful human medicines, Lasix was soon used on horses. It proved to be useful for the treatment of animals who retained fluid in the lungs after a bout with respiratory disease. But Lasix had a couple of side effects that made racing officials worry about its potential abuse:

➤ Because it increased urine flow, there was the danger that Lasix might mask the presence of other drugs in post-race tests.

➤ Because it appeared to improve lung capacity in sick horses, there was the danger that it might improve healthy horses, too. Lung capacity is part of the physical package that makes a good racehorse.

But Lasix proved to have one side effect that far outweighs everything else for racing people. It appears to reduce the incidence of bleeding from the lungs, the great scourge of the modern Thoroughbred racehorse.

Bleeding—its proper name is *exercise-induced pulmonary hemorrhage* (EIPH)—worries all horse people. Bleeding involves the rupture of tiny blood vessels in the lungs, and it's extraordinarily common. Some horsemen believe that most Thoroughbreds would show evidence of blood in the lungs or trachea after every race if they were all examined internally.

Inside Track

If you hear a horse called a bleeder, he's one who suffers so badly that blood is visible and his performance is clearly affected. His past performance line may show that he stopped suddenly, followed by the word *bled*.

Bleeding is prompted by strenuous exercise, particularly at high speed. These horses are often affected:

➤ Quarter Horses, particularly those older than two or three.

➤ Thoroughbreds, particularly sprinters and middle-distance horses.

These horses are less affected:

➤ Steeplechasers, because the speed demanded of them is less what's required for racing on the flat.

➤ Standardbreds, although there is some bleeding among horses who race under harness.

Some racing jurisdictions require horses to bleed in the presence of a veterinarian before they can use Lasix. Others allow the drug for a horse whose bleeding has never been seen by anyone. At racetracks in those states, you may see every horse in the race with an *L* next to his name. Trainers even find it worthwhile to ship a nonvisible bleeder to a permissive state to establish a Lasix history.

Bad Bet

Remember that a horse who's been put on Lasix because of a serious bleeding incident in a race or workout is more likely than most other horses to bleed badly again. He won't be a good bet, no matter what drug he's given.

Just why is Lasix so popular? It's twice as expensive as bute, and it doesn't always work, especially among serious bleeders. Here's a fact that used to be a well-whispered secret among trainers and bettors: Lasix appears to make almost all horses run a little faster.

The effect is greatest the first time a horse races with Lasix, although some improvement continues in later races. The importance of first-time Lasix use is so great that entry lists almost always include, in addition to the L for Lasix, a special notation for first-time users. This notation is usually the symbol *L1*. An L1 horse is worth serious consideration because of the likelihood of improvement.

Are They Drugs or Are They Treatments?

A few other treatments may or may not help horses run faster. Some are illegal, some are frowned upon, and some don't show up in current tests, making regulation difficult. These two are the most common:

➤ *Jugs* are injections of a solution of substances into a horse's jugular vein just before the race. Jugs usually include vitamins, amino acids, minerals, and possibly a trainer's secret substance. It's believed that the jug has more effect than the same substance fed to the horse because it goes immediately to the bloodstream. A lot of trainers and tipsters swear by jugs, but there's no real proof yet.

➤ *Milk shakes* are also used, illegally in some areas, to improve racing performance. No, they're not the beverage you use to wash down your hamburger, but rather a sodium bicarbonate solution not much different from the antacid you take after you eat that hamburger. The logic is this: Sodium bicarbonate is supposed to neutralize the lactic acid that builds up in muscles, causing fatigue and muscle pain. The lactic acid buildup is most intense in high-speed, mid-distance races. Milk shakes became especially popular in one-mile Standardbred racing, at least until racing authorities noticed.

Testing

There's a pervasive belief among racing skeptics that the testing laboratories are far behind the chemists creating new drugs and even farther behind people willing to use the drugs unethically. They point to the fact that less than one percent of the samples tested nationwide each year come back positive.

The truth is this: The labs are behind, and scientists admit that several dozen equine drugs simply don't show up in current tests. An industry-wide effort is underway to catch up to modern chemistry. There's also the very practical trend to save for future tests blood and urine samples from suspicious cases that don't show anything under current testing procedures.

The procedures vary from state to state, but usually the winner (or all placed horses) is required to give post-race urine samples. Beaten favorites are also tested, as is any horse whose performance stood out as too good or too bad to be true. Random finishers are also selected for testing.

Most jurisdictions split the samples, saving some for retesting should the first test come up positive. Others do two tests on every sample. Some split only a few randomly chosen samples; others do blind testing for quality assurance.

When a positive to an identifiable illegal drug is discovered, the information is relayed to the racetrack, usually a few days after the race. The horse is disqualified, the purse is redistributed, and the trainer usually gets suspended.

The length of the suspension depends on the drug; long penalties are imposed for the discovery of one of the drugs with no known therapeutic value.

The betting results are not changed, and this invariably infuriates the holders of tickets on losing horses. Disgruntled bettors have taken their cases to court, but so far, this policy has not changed.

Chapter 4

Age, Sex, and Other Ways to Discriminate

In This Chapter

➤ Why older is usually better among racehorses

➤ The equine battle of the sexes

➤ Brains versus brawn among racehorses

➤ The angry or nervous horse

You might think that age would be a straightforward element of race analysis. You read the horse's age as it's printed in the program, think about what it could mean to the race, and then make your decision about his chances. Unfortunately, the age issue is not always quite so clear, and the confusion starts early.

All racehorses have the same birthday even though it's possible for a horse to be born any day of the year. On New Year's Day, every horse born during the previous year celebrates its first birthday, whether he's ten months, six months, or one day old. The next January 1, he becomes a two-year-old, and so on. The difference between the official birthday and the real one is important in all two-year-old racing and in three-year-old racing, at least until September.

Breeders do their best to make sure their foals are born as soon after January 1 as possible (a December 31 foal is a disaster), but luck and scheduling sometimes see foals born in June or even July. A two-year-old race scheduled before June is likely to include one or more *yearlings*.

From the Horse's Mouth

A **yearling** is a one-year-old horse.

Many past performance publications and track programs help you identify the chronological yearlings in two-year-old races by printing the month of birth after each horse's breeding line. This information is also occasionally given for three-year-old races so you can pick out the chronological two-year-olds there.

Age matters to betting decisions, but just a little. The birth month isn't a magical dividing line. A horse too young to race well the day before his real birthday isn't going to be automatically mature enough the day after. Consider the birth months of two-year-olds a loose guideline.

A very late birthdate—especially if this race is scheduled early in the year—should be considered a mark against the horse as you make your betting decisions. Conversely, an early birthdate gives a horse an advantage in physical and mental development.

Inside Track

Among horses as well as people, females mature a little earlier. Two-year-old females tend to be more ready to race than males of the same age.

Do remember that each horse matures at a slightly different rate. Some very young horses, even chronological yearlings, are ready to race, and horses several months older are not. But, in general, older is better for two- and three-year-olds. Throughout those years, horses grow in height, gain more bone density, and develop bigger muscles.

What's in a Name

Some birthdays give a horse a whole new name. What you call a horse depends on age, sex, and sport.

➤ In all racing breeds, two- and three-year-old males are *colts*. Two- and three-year-old females are *fillies,* although you'll occasionally come across old-timers who don't use the word *filly*. To them, all females are *mares*.

➤ With Standardbreds and Quarter Horses, four-year-old males become *stallions,* and four-year-old females become mares. They retain these names for the rest of their lives.

➤ At four, Thoroughbreds are still colts, becoming stallions at the age of five. Fillies are fillies at four, becoming mares at the age of five.

➤ Standardbreds and Quarter Horses of both sexes are officially described as aged after their three-year-old seasons, although they are still also stallions and mares.

➤ Thoroughbreds are never officially aged, but you may use that word to refer to a really elderly horse.

➤ In all three breeds, *geldings* are called geldings from the day of their surgery. They are no longer colts, even if they are babies.

From the Horse's Mouth

Geldings are castrated male horses. They usually undergo the operation as yearlings or two-year-olds, but it can be done at any time. Gelded males usually concentrate on their racing careers better than stallions, so the operation is almost always done on young male horses who are not likely to be in demand as stallions.

When Age Matters

In racing, age matters most when horses are very young or very old. What's old is relative. In most other horse sports, a horse under the age of six is a mere baby, far too young to excel. In these sports, horses can be competitive into their late teens.

In racing, however, most horses are at their best from the second half of their three-year-old season through their five-year-old season. But they do race long before and after that two-and-a-half-year season, and you should try to understand what age means to the not-quite-prime competitors.

Two-Year-Olds

One aspect of two-year-old racing makes it easier for bettors, at least those wagering on Thoroughbreds and Quarter Horses. Two-year-olds race shorter distances than most other horses, especially early in the year. You don't have to fit stamina into the equation. Speed is all.

In Thoroughbred racing, two-year-olds race at 4 and 5 furlongs early in the year, stretching to 6 to 7 furlongs as summer progresses. In the fall, there are a few mile and $1^1/_{16}$ mile races for two-year-olds at the bigger racetracks.

In Quarter Horse racing, two-year-olds start at 220 yards early in the year, never going more than 440. Standard-bred two-year-olds race at one mile, like older horses.

If you want to bet on two-year-old races, follow the guidelines in Chapter 2 to identify speed. Then keep in mind the following facts about two-year-olds:

➤ **They have to learn how to race.** Workouts, even in the company of other horses, can't simulate the cavalry-charge nature of real racing. Some horses become frightened; others are thrilled by the competition. Each kind makes mistakes: running too fast, slowing up, ducking in, or drifting out.

➤ **Experience counts.** Horses with even a little experience are more likely to win than first-time starters, but even they will experience things in your race that they've never seen before. They probably will be a little quicker to adjust than a first-time starter, but not necessarily.

The Older Horse

At the other end of the age spectrum are the older horses. Racehorses are a little like supermodels. They're branded as too old just as they are reaching full maturity.

In racing, it's not just prejudice. Because of the physical stress caused by pounding on racetracks, horses' legs age much more quickly than the rest of them. By the time they reach the age of six, most racehorses have old legs. Just how old depends on how many times a horse has started, the kind of surface he's been racing on, and how fast he runs. *Turf horses* tend to last a little longer, as do distance runners and Standardbreds.

From the Horse's Mouth

Turf horses race over grass courses rather than dirt tracks. Some horses do both, but most are better on one than the other.

Occasionally, a horse that is extremely sound to begin with can win at sprint distances on hard dirt tracks when he's well past the age of six. He should be worshipped as well as bet on.

Sex

Most races are segregated by sex. Fillies and mares are permitted to run in most races, but other races are scheduled exclusively for them. There is a widely held belief among most people involved in racing that female horses aren't quite as good at racing as males. Sometimes they are, and sometimes they aren't.

What they are is different. Even in their own races, fillies and mares require a little extra analysis before you bet on them. Most observers believe that female horses can run or trot as fast as male horses of similar class (pacing is different). What the females often lack are some of the other qualities that contribute to winning, primarily consistency. The lack of consistency can be between races or even within a single race. The villain is hormones. (Stallions are affected by hormones, too, but a surge of testosterone seems to help a stallion run better, bulling his way to the lead and fighting off the opposition.)

When betting on fillies and mares, heat periods (internal, not meteorological) are what you have to watch for. Fillies start coming into heat in the spring of their two-year-old years, and most continue with heat periods until they die. A few mares have heat periods year-round, but most only cycle from late winter to late summer. Many fillies and mares run their best races during the cold weather of fall and winter.

Heats come as often as every two weeks and can last three to five days. During these spells, female horses might pay more attention to the siren song of their hormones than anything else in their lives. This causes the inconsistency on the racetrack, a characteristic most pronounced if male horses are on the track. Even geldings become attractive to a mare in heat.

Inside Track

You can sometimes spot a mare in heat as she's saddled for a race or as she is parading to the post. She may lift her tail, dance around, and be generally unprofessional.

Some mares run fast as ever during their heats; others can't outrace their own shadows. They are probably hoping their shadows have turned male. Some trainers give their mares a drug with the trade name Regumate™ during the spring and summer to suppress heat periods. These mares should run normally, but the drug isn't reported, and you will have no way of knowing about it.

Here are some other factors to consider when betting on fillies and mares:

> ➤ **Age.** Two-year-olds are more competitive with males than other fillies and mares are, possibly because their heats are both less intense and don't come quite so often. It may also be because females mature more quickly than males.

> ➤ **Distance.** Among running horses, females are most competitive with males over sprint distances, probably because of the advantage of wider hips in sprinting. They are also very competitive over distances of a mile and a half and up, probably because they have less body weight to haul around the racetrack.

> ➤ **Gait.** Among Standardbreds, trotting females are probably equal to males. It's hard to know for sure because good ones are kept in female-only races. Among pacers, males are clearly superior to females of similar class. The wider hips of fillies and mares are an advantage at the trot and a disadvantage at the pace.

Courage

Courage is the most admired quality in a racehorse, although it's certainly less useful than speed and soundness. But courage can make a difference in individual races, and it can surely make you enjoy watching your horse run if he displays it.

From the Horse's Mouth

You'll often hear a brave racehorse referred to as **game.**

Racehorse courage usually comes in the form of willingness to make an effort in spite of pain, whether the pain comes from the lungs at the end of a long, demanding race or whether it comes from legs hurting from injury, age, or too much racing.

Some horses show incredible courage, often with little common sense to go along with it. Racehorse courage might show up like this:

➤ A horse that holds on to his position in spite of challenges from fresher or even faster horses.

➤ A horse who allows himself to be urged into an opening between horses that's a little narrower than he is.

➤ Every horse that is competitive and runs a respectable race, even though his legs and muscles feel the wear and tear of too much racing.

You identify these horses in the past performance charts.

Temperament

Bad-tempered horses are dangerous to the people who work with them, as well as to other horses. If they're not so temperamental that they can't be forced to follow racing procedures, they can give good accountings of themselves on the racetracks.

From the Horse's Mouth

The **stewards** are the policemen, judge, and jury of the racetrack, enforcing rules and making decisions about eligibility and results. They can order bad actors off the track until they learn to behave.

Here's how you spot the bad actors:

➤ They fight and kick when they're saddled or harnessed.

➤ After the rider or driver is up, they fight human control.

➤ They have to be isolated from other horses to prevent possible injury from kicking or biting.

➤ They are difficult to load into the starting gate, or they refuse to line up behind it if they are Standardbreds.

Some horses are nervous rather than angry, but they, too, can expend so much energy before the start that they don't have enough left to race effectively. Avoid the following:

➤ Horses who work themselves into a sweaty lather of tension, unless the day is so hot that every horse is sweating.

➤ Horses so upset by the sights around the track that they jump and hop their way through the post parade.

➤ Horses that seem to be afraid of the crowd.

Chapter 5

The Well-Equipped Horse

In This Chapter

➤ How changes of equipment affect races

➤ What equipment is most important to racing performance

➤ Recognizing what matters

The bettor must deal with the racehorse trainer's apparently limitless desire to tinker with existing equipment—adding, subtracting, combining, altering, and otherwise adjusting what goes onto the horse.

Shoes

As important as a horse's feet are to racing success, there is a limit to what even the most inventive trainer can do with them. Running horses don't wear anything other than horseshoes. The Standardbred wears *boots* as well as shoes, but the fancy footwear usually protects him from himself rather than makes him faster.

From the Horse's Mouth

Horse **boots** consist of cups, pads, wraps, and other devices that are placed on and around a horse's leg. They are not pulled up over his feet.

Thoroughbreds and Quarter Horses normally race in extremely light, all-aluminum horseshoes called *racing plates*. Most are plain, but some trainers experiment with shoes intended to increase support or traction for horses who seem a little too tentative in their strides. These shoes are not reported to the public and cannot be figured into race analysis.

But a shoe designed specifically for racing on muddy tracks does have to be reported at almost every racetrack. Its use is important to watch for when it rains. The shoe is the *mud caulk,* better known around the racetrack as the *sticker.*

Deciding whether to use stickers keeps trainers awake when they hear rain pattering on the roof. Why don't all trainers use stickers when it rains? For the following reasons:

➤ Skid is normal and desirable. It allows the tendons and ligaments to absorb and distribute some of the stress and shock of the ground strike. If the hoof sticks too much, nothing gives, and catastrophic injury can result.

➤ Mud caulks are heavier than flat racing plates, and every ounce counts for the running horse.

➤ The decision to use them usually has to be made the day of the race and that means reshoeing shortly before race time. Nails have to be pulled and reinserted, creating the risk of chipping the horny part of the hoof or pricking living tissue. Either can cause temporary lameness and defeat.

To bet on *off-track* races, you must mirror the trainer's decision-making process, except that you have one advantage. You can watch a race or two over the track, including the race right before the one you're interested in. The trainer usually can't wait quite so long to make his decision.

From the Horse's Mouth

An **off track** is one that isn't dry and fast. It can range from slightly damp to brown soup.

If you have a sharp eye, you can assess how the horses are reacting to an off track:

➤ You can see some horses show their insecurity with the footing by shortening their strides.

➤ You can see some horses appear to climb with their front legs.

➤ You can see some jockeys make their moves to the inside or outside more tentatively than they do on a dry track.

Inside Track

Always bring binoculars to the racetrack so you can
examine things such as footing and equipment. If you're at
a simulcast facility, get as close as you can to the screen.

Standardbreds and Shoes

Shoeing is a little different for harness racing because the
choice of shoe affects gait as well as traction. Shoes with
small projections, known as *grabs,* are used even on dry
tracks when a trainer thinks his horse's gait will become
smoother or faster if his feet don't slide quite so much.
Trainers are less likely to be concerned about traction on
off tracks because harness tracks have less cushion and
don't get nearly as muddy as running tracks do.

Standardbred trainers also worry about the weight of their
horses' shoes because an ounce or two more or less in any
one of the four shoes can change a horse's stride. Heavier
shoes, particularly in front, make some harness horses
stride out more, extending their gaits. A heavier shoe on
one foot can balance an uneven gait.

Standardbred trainers do a great deal of experimenting
with shoeing, far more than trainers in any other equine
sport. You'll hear about very little of it unless you have
a contact at the stable. But Standardbreds race often,
sometimes once a week, and you occasionally can spot
a horse whose trainer has discovered the right shoeing
combination. He may be the one who shows a sudden
improvement over his last race.

Horse Headwear

A horse may race with his legs, lungs, and heart, but his head carries a greater variety of equipment than any of the more critical parts. Most of the items are used to calm and control tense competitors. We'll look first at the equipment worn by running horses.

Blinkers

The first course of treatment for a horse whose mental efforts fall short is a pair of blinkers. Blinkers are used on these animals:

➤ Horses that are distracted by other horses.

➤ Horses that become nervous at the sight of spectators.

➤ Horses that are inclined to see ghosts.

Being outfitted with blinkers is the racehorse's equivalent of having your seat changed by the teacher so you don't pass notes to your friends during English class.

Thoroughbred and Quarter Horse blinkers consist of a light cotton or synthetic hood that's placed over the horse's head and fastened under his jowls with Velcro, snaps, or buckles. Holes are cut out for the ears and eyes.

A plastic or leather cup is fastened to the back edge of each eye hole, restricting the wearer's peripheral vision. The cup may be less than an inch wide, limiting the horse's view only slightly, or it may be two inches or more, allowing the horse to see only directly in front of him. The cup may almost completely cover the eye, but it may have a slit cut out in back so the horse can see behind but not what's directly next to him. You will also see blinkers in which the cups differ on each side.

Bad Bet

Blinkers with big, closed cups can lose a race for a horse who doesn't notice another horse coming up alongside in deep stretch. By the time he sees the competition, it's past him.

Changes involving blinkers are made public before a race, and it's done for good reason. Some horses behave even worse with them than without. The first use of blinkers is always an experiment, and the horse should be bet on with caution.

Shadow Rolls

A large, soft roll of sheepskin or synthetic material over the noseband of the bridle also helps prevent distraction. It's called a shadow roll and was developed to discourage horses from thinking that their own shadows are barriers that require a jump or a zigzag.

Shadow rolls are especially useful in night racing because the lighting comes from several directions and creates unfamiliar shadows. But some trainers use shadow rolls even on cloudy days, believing that racehorses are more likely to pay attention to their jockeys and respond to their urging when they can't look down under their own feet.

The use of shadow rolls isn't reported to the public, so you have to rely on your own powers of observation. If you notice a horse without a shadow roll jump or move suddenly right or left for no reason, watch to see whether a shadow roll is added next time he starts. This little piece of sheepskin may be enough to turn a loser into a winner.

The Bridle

Most horses race in a simple snaffle bit consisting of a metal bar that goes through the mouth and is connected to the straps of the bridle by round or D-shaped rings on each side of the face. The bar is jointed in the middle, a design that lessens the pressure on the sides of the mouth that occurs when the jockey steers.

The snaffle is a mild bit, but some horses need more control. Rather than making the bit more severe and risking injury to the horse's mouth, the trainer of a difficult horse is likely to try a bridle with straps that cross over each other in the middle of the nose. Racing people call this arrangement a figure-8. It helps prevent a strong horse from pulling, evading the bit, or otherwise ignoring his jockey's orders.

Like the shadow roll, the figure-8's use isn't reported to the public, but its presence is obvious to anyone who looks. If you spot a horse with a regular straight noseband (or no noseband at all) and notice that pulling or fighting seems to contribute to his defeat, watch him next time. If he's sporting a figure-8, it may make the difference.

Tongue Ties

Some racehorses allow their tongues to slip back in their mouths, partially blocking their air passages. A horse who does this is said to swallow his tongue, although he's really just allowing loose flesh to clog up the works. The tongue stays in the mouth.

Swallowing the tongue rarely does more than slow the horse down, but occasionally a horse collapses on the track because of it. To prevent this from happening, almost every Thoroughbred wears a tongue tie, a stretchy white ribbon that ties the tongue to the lower jaw so it can't slip back.

Horses don't seem to mind tongue ties, and trainers would rather be safe than sorry. Tongue ties are now so common that they don't figure into betting decisions.

The Saddle

There's been little experimentation in saddle design since the turn of the last century. The changes don't involve saddle shape but rather the weight that's added to make up the difference between the jockey and weight assignments. Every horse who starts in the Kentucky Derby, for example, will most likely carry some of his assigned 126 pounds in the form of added weight. Even more ordinary horses are likely to carry added weight if they're ridden by lightweight jockeys.

Traditionally, bars of lead have been used, either inserted in slots in the saddle or in pads under the saddle. A bettor can't know whether a horse is carrying comfortable pads or unpleasant lead bars, but it's a good bet that the pads will become the rule rather than the exception in the future. Assigned weight may then become less of a burden.

Harness Racing Equipment

Standardbreds carry considerably more equipment than running horses. This extra equipment offers plenty of opportunity for trainers to experiment.

Sulky

The most dramatic and visible change in harness racing during the 20th century has been in the vehicle pulled by the horse, known as the *sulky* or *racebike*. Look at Currier & Ives harness racing prints from the mid–19th century, and you'll see ponderous, high-wheeled carts. The wheels began to shrink late in the century, evolving into a small, light design with bicycle-style wheels.

The traditional sulky dominated the sport until the late 1960s, when a modified vehicle appeared. The new sulky placed the driver's weight behind the wheels rather than over them, allowing the horse to move more freely. The modified sulky was clearly faster than the old sulky and became the vehicle of choice.

Design experimentation continued. Among the new sulkies that appeared was one that featured bent *shafts,* and it appeared to almost everyone to be faster than the now-conventional modified vehicle. But racing officials decided that the bent-shaft sulky is potentially unsafe, and it was banned from most racetracks.

From the Horse's Mouth

The **shafts** are the poles that attach the sulky to the horse's harness.

That ban has been in the courts for several years, so the bent-shaft sulky may not have disappeared forever from all tracks. If it's used at a track you attend, note that some experts are convinced that it leads to substantially faster times for the horses that pull it.

Equipment for Gaiting

Almost all pacers wear *hopples,* sometimes called *hobbles,* to help them maintain their gait. These plastic loops make it easier for a horse to go into the pace from a walk and help prevent him from breaking into a *gallop* from the pace.

From the Horse's Mouth

The **gallop** is the horse's fastest gait. A good gallop is cherished in Thoroughbreds and Quarter Horses and dreaded in a Standardbred because he has to be pulled out of contention if he breaks into one.

If you go to the harness track enough times, you may someday see a free-legged pacer. Figure him this way: If the trainer thinks the horse can stay on gait without hopples, he probably can.

Trotters, who are more likely to break out of stride anyway, don't get as much help from equipment. There are half hopples that go around only the front legs and some new four-legged trotting hopples, but the jury is still out on whether they help to keep a horse *flat.*

From the Horse's Mouth

A trotter who stays **flat** keeps trotting rather than breaking into a gallop.

Some trainers and drivers think that *head poles* or *gaiting poles,* which run alongside the horse's shoulder and neck, help some horses to stay on stride. They force the horse to keep his body straight, and a horse usually has to bend a little to break into a gallop.

Harness

At its simplest, the harness is nothing more than a device to attach the sulky to the horse, but it also provides the framework to add or subtract other items of equipment, most of which are designed to improve the balance and ease of the stride. Among the equipment you may see:

➤ A strap that attaches the horse's head to another strap that goes around his chest, keeping the horse from raising his head. This strap is called a *martingale.*

➤ A strap that attaches the horse's head to the top of his back, preventing him from lowering his head. This strap is called an *overcheck* or a *checkrein.*

➤ Boots and bandages, all designed to protect the horse's flesh from being struck by his own feet. These include bell boots on his hoofs, knee boots, elbow boots, and protective bandages on any or all cannon bones. A horse that wears boots probably needs them, but boots distract and probably slow horses down at least a little.

Standardbreds use blinkers and shadow rolls for the same reasons running horses do. They also commonly use blind or closed bridles, which include leather or plastic flaps next to the eye. A few Standardbreds are equipped with earmuffs if the sound of the crowd distracts them. Occasionally, you'll see Thoroughbreds with ear coverings, but they're primarily used on harness horses.

Probably fewer than half of all Standardbreds race with open bridles and no shadow rolls, even though they tend to concentrate better and behave more calmly than Thoroughbreds. Conventional wisdom says that driving horses fear the sight of their own vehicles behind them, so the widespread use of closed bridles may be as much a remnant of tradition as a concern about distractions.

Chapter 6

The Hands That Hold the Reins: The Jockeys

There's no doubt that a rider can make a winner into a loser. He can also make a loser into a winner, although it's a little more difficult. In the vast majority of races, however, the rider's impact on the outcome is only minor. The horse makes the difference, not the human.

Who Are the Little Big Men?

There's an inherent contradiction in every jockey, a contradiction so profound that it seems surprising that jockeys can exist at all. Riders of racehorses have to be very light and very strong at the same time, a combination remarkably difficult to find in the same person. To be able to ride inmost *flat races,* a jockey can't weigh much more than 110 pounds (steeplechase riders can be heavier, perhaps 140 pounds).

From the Horse's Mouth

A **flat race** is one without jumps.

At 110 pounds, he or she can carry a couple pounds' worth of saddle and still come in at the assigned weight for the average horse in the average race. That's not much body weight for an adult male who has to be in good enough health to perform a difficult, demanding athletic task.

Inside Track

An announced overweight horse can sometimes be a very good bet. The fact that the trainer didn't switch to another jockey shows that he has enough confidence in both horse and jockey not to make a change to get the extra help of a little less weight.

At the same time that he has to be light, the jockey has to have considerable upper-body strength. A Thoroughbred or Quarter Horse usually weighs at least half a ton, is young and energetic, and is only minimally trained to stop and steer. Some racehorses respond to gentle cues and finesse, but others need pure power to keep them where they are supposed to be.

Jockeys need muscles, something that contributes mightily to body weight, so jockeys make up for that extra weight by being short, sometimes very short. You'll rarely see a male jockey taller than about 5 feet 4 inches.

Female Jockeys

When the first female jockeys were licensed in the late 1960s, some people believed that they would come to dominate the profession. They thought that women light enough and short enough to ride would be easier to find than men of similar body size. What was abnormally small for a man would be common and average for a woman.

Naysayers said that female jockeys would never succeed in any great numbers because most lack upper body strength. Thirty years later, the second group seems to be right, although comparative upper body strength is only part of the reason.

Among female jockeys, only Julie Krone reached and stayed in the very top echelon of riders. There are more women who inhabit the upper-middle range and make a very good living at race riding, but very few women ride in the big stakes races, the Triple Crown and the Breeders' Cup, possibly because the trainers fear lack of strength.

The shortage of rides limits the amount of experience that female jockeys can get, prompting even more trainers to avoid them. A bettor doesn't have to avoid a female jockey, but her experience and strength should be considered if they appear to play a role in a particular race. If she doesn't get many rides, consider her like any other inexperienced jockey.

The Apprentice Jockey

Weight and riding success are most closely entwined during the first year of a jockey's career. For that year, the jockey is considered an apprentice, a kind of working student. Given the competitiveness of racing, the young jockey would get almost no chance to race if he or she weren't given a special break.

From the Horse's Mouth

Apprentice jockeys are sometimes called **bug boys** even if they're girls. The phrase refers to the asterisk often used next to their names. A **journeyman jockey** is one who has completed his apprentice year.

Trainers are encouraged to use apprentice jockeys by being given a weight break for their horses. The weight allowance is scaled to give the greatest break to the most inexperienced jockeys. There are variations in different racing jurisdictions, but here's a typical scale chart:

Apprentice Allowances

Jockey's wins	Weight off assigned impost
0-5	10 pounds
6-35	7 pounds
For 1 year after 5th win	5 pounds

The allowance guarantees that some trainers will use apprentice jockeys on horses who need a low weight to have a chance, and it almost guarantees that an apprentice with natural talent will win a lot of races in spite of inexperience.

Inside Track

Apprentices don't get the weight break in stakes races. If they get the mount anyway, the trainer thinks the rider really suits the horse. That's a plus.

For the racegoer, a poor-to-average apprentice is not usually much of a bet, unless he's been given a horse with excellent credentials (unlikely, unless the horse really needs a weight break). But a horse with an apprentice who has won dozens of races can be judged like any other horse-rider combination. The weight will be a plus, and the rider's experience level will be a slight (but just a slight) negative.

Riding Skills

Jockeys must bring a few basic skills to the race. They have to stay aboard, and they have to be able to steer. You can safely assume that a jockey who's made a number of starts will do both adequately. Trainers wouldn't use him otherwise.

Inside Track

If you see that a famous jockey has worked an unraced or lightly raced horse, you can be sure that he thinks the horse is worth his time. It's a horse to watch and maybe bet on.

The break from the starting gate is the single most important event in a Quarter Horse race as well as in any Thoroughbred race of 6 furlongs or less. In short races, there isn't enough time or yardage to make up for a bad start. There's hardly enough to make up for a so-so start, even with a clearly superior horse. Its importance decreases as distance increases, but there's no race, including a three-mile steeplechase, in which the start isn't important.

A jockey who gets the jump on other riders is alert, not psychic. He doesn't so much anticipate the start as have himself and his horse ready the very second the starter chooses to open the gate.

Most horses are tense in the starting gate because they're imprisoned in a space only a few inches larger than their own bodies. A good gate jockey has to exert a calming influence on the horse as well as being alert. Like lightness and strength, the ability to be relaxed and the ability to be alert often don't exist in the same person.

There are no charts that list jockeys who break well from the gate, but you can often identify them on the past performance charts. These charts, as you'll see later, show the horse's position at various points in the race.

The results charts from the previous day's racing also report how the horses broke from the gate. Using yesterday's results won't tell you how today's horses are going to break, but you can use them to identify the riders who break effectively.

As you examine both sets of charts, you'll find the names of some riders who always seem to be in the first three or four out of the gate. Having one of these jockeys will be a big plus for a horse in a short race, and it certainly won't hurt one in a longer event.

Timing

A sense of timing is second in importance only to the start for a Thoroughbred jockey. It's not nearly as important in Quarter Horse racing, where there's one *pace*—all out. In Thoroughbred racing, even in very short events, horses differ in where they like to run.

From the Horse's Mouth

The **pace** is the speed of the horse or horses in the lead.

Some horses prefer to be in front from the start; others would rather make their runs from behind. The jockey has to control how fast the horse is permitted to run while in front or when he should start his run from off the pace. Horses who run too fast on the lead don't last, and those who make their moves too late never get there.

Good timing can be hard to identify. It shows up primarily in the form of a high winning percentage. Even then, it's difficult to know if a horse wins because of its own superiority or because the jockey was good at judging the pace of the race.

Some observers believe that a rider who finishes second and third often but rarely wins has the physical skills to be a good jockey but lacks a sense of timing. He may actually be an outstanding jockey, if those second- and third-place horses finish as close as they do because he gets the most out of them.

If you think that raw results don't tell you enough, you can also examine past performance and results charts to assess riders' timing. Look for signs that a jockey, once he has allowed his horse to take the lead, manages to keep him near the front all the way to the finish. Or you want to see that a rider coming from behind makes his move at a point where the horse neither runs out of racetrack nor energy before the finish. He doesn't have to win, but you want to see him in contention at the finish line.

Turf Racing

Outstanding jockeys are usually outstanding regardless of the surface they race on, whether it's hard and dry or soft and muddy. Most of them are also good on turf, but certain jockeys seem to shine in turf racing. Here's why:

➤ Turf courses are usually smaller and have sharper turns than their adjacent dirt tracks. Jockeys who understand the need to get out of the gate quickly and to be well placed by the first turn excel on the turf, even in longer races where they don't need an early lead.

➤ Early speed usually doesn't hold up quite so well on the turf as it does on the dirt, so jockeys with a good sense of timing and pace when coming from behind are often very effective on the turf.

➤ Turf courses can't be groomed as easily as dirt tracks and are more inclined to develop bad spots. Jockeys who are good at placing horses where they want them to be rather than allowing others to dictate do well on the turf.

How do you identify these turf experts? The same way you identify jockeys with other important skills. You study past performance charts and daily results. With turf racing, you have additional tools.

Chapter 7

The Other Hands That Hold the Reins: The Drivers

In This Chapter

➤ Driving skills

➤ Identifying the good driver

The driver of a Standardbred racehorse is more important and plays a bigger role in the outcome of the race than does the rider of a Thoroughbred or a Quarter Horse. Ironically, he's more important, at least in part, because driving is easier.

Most Standardbreds are calm, quiet, and well-behaved. Most flat runners are not. Drivers, not having to concentrate on staying aboard while getting the horse into the gate, out of the gate, and into a more or less straight line, can usually focus on strategy and tactics throughout the race. Jockeys are more often along for the ride. Some jockeys do make tactical decisions, and some drivers just go along with the flow, but the comparative importance of the human participant is different in each sport.

You'll hear different estimates of the relative contributions. In flat racing, you'll find the consensus somewhere around 90 to 95 percent horse, 5 to 10 percent human. The figures are a little closer in harness racing, but you'd be hard-pressed to find anybody who thinks the horse is less than 75 to 80 percent responsible for whether he wins or loses. In both sports, the horse is still most of the race, but you can't ignore the hands on the reins in either sport.

Driving Skills

Identifying the drivers with the most important skills helps you to share in their wins. Here's what's important.

Leaving

Racing quickly from the start is called *leaving,* and the driver who does it well is going to be both admired and successful. Everybody leaves now, but not everybody does it equally well.

From the Horse's Mouth

The **wire** is the finish line, even though there's rarely either a wire or a line. Instead, it's a marker on a judge's stand in the infield of the track. You're supposed to imagine the line.

Figure the odds. If everybody leaves, hoping to get to or near the front, most are going to lose out. The loser will be the driver who hasn't adequately assessed his horse's early speed, who hasn't gotten his horse sufficiently alert, or who lacks the aggressiveness to stake a claim on track position and hold onto it no matter what.

Bad Bet

Leaving can be dangerous when it turns into the aborted leave, where the horse gets moving quickly but has to be taken back suddenly because there's no space for him. He wastes energy and loses position at the same time.

By the first turn, a driver good at leaving usually manages to get his horse to the rail, or just one horse out, without finding himself behind a wall of horses. Leaving well is more important on the $1/2$-mile and $5/8$-mile tracks than on the 1-mile tracks. We'll get into track size more in Chapter 8.

Timing the Move

Except perhaps for the superstars who set their own rules, no horse can maintain top speed on the lead for an entire race. A good driver knows when to ask for speed and when to ease off.

A driver can actually be too good at this. Some drivers understand pace so well that they used to ask their horses to leave, and then settled back on the lead at such a slow pace that the field of horses would seem to be crawling around the track. The leading driver, whose horse retained plenty of energy, would then ask for speed in the final quarter. Nobody could catch him.

The smart strategists prospered, as did people who bet on them, but fans (including those who bet on the other horses) despised the technique. The so-called *slow quarter rule* now prohibits this practice. This rule is the harness racing equivalent of a shot clock, eliminating any deliberate slowdowns. The horse can be disqualified and the driver suspended if he's guilty of racing any quarter too slowly.

Avoiding Trouble

Good drivers seem to be able to keep themselves and their horses out of situations that lose races. Foremost is the ability to avoid being *parked.*

Inside Track

An occasional horse races well parked, even preferring it, possibly because he doesn't like horses on his right side. But he usually isn't a good bet because his driver will not want to be embarrassed by racing parked. He'll probably force the horse near to the rail, where he will lose.

No, being parked doesn't involve stopping and standing. In fact, if you're parked you have to work even harder than you would if you avoided this catastrophe. Being parked is being forced wide. It's undesirable in any racing sport, but in harness racing it can be a disaster. Sharp turns and the extra width of the sulky make being parked a very difficult obstacle to overcome in any race. A driver who usually manages to avoid it is worth following and often betting on.

Trouble also comes when a driver is forced to take evasive action because a horse directly in front of him suddenly slows down. This situation happens often because racing directly behind another horse is good strategy. It's called *racing under cover,* and it allows a horse to move quickly without expending much energy. Racing under cover follows the same principle as slipstreaming in auto racing. A good driver knows whether the horse he's racing behind is likely to slow suddenly; a not-so-good driver is happily oblivious until he unhappily has to pull his horse up to avoid an accident.

Measures of Success

Track programs and racing publications give you different lists of successful drivers. You may find lists of drivers whose horses:

➤ Have won the most money.

➤ Have won the most dashes (individual races).

➤ Have won the most races in less than 2:00 or less than 1:55.

➤ Have finished in the first three most often.

More useful than any list is an effective tool dreamed up by the harness sport. It's the *Universal Driver Rating System,* commonly called the *UDR,* a statistic designed to identify the drivers most likely to give you a run (or rather a trot or pace) for your money.

The UDR looks like a batting average, but it's more elaborate than a simple placing percentage. The rating gives the most weight to a win, next most to a second-place finish, and a little credit for a third. Unplaced finishes, even close ones, get no statistical consideration.

Any UDR above .300 is good, with a couple of caveats. A UDR based on only a few starts, perhaps at the start of a year or the early days of a race meet, is statistically invalid.

A great driver may have goose eggs, and a poor one may be batting a thousand.

Also look at past performance and results charts for the drivers whose horses are in good position after a quarter, whose performance lines show that they are rarely parked, and who hold their positions or improve in the final quarter.

Newcomers

Racing programs inform you if a driver is less than fully experienced. The letter *P* in a circle, the sign of a *provisional driver,* appears next to his or her name.

From the Horse's Mouth

A **provisional driver** is one who has raced less than a year and has had fewer than 25 starts in betting races.

You'll occasionally see an *A* for amateur or an *F* for a driver licensed to race only at fair meets. All of these symbols count against the horse when you're trying to pick a winner.

Catch Driver Versus Trainer/Driver

At any major track today, the horse you bet on is probably handled by a person who neither trains nor owns the horse he's driving. Fifteen years ago, you would have seen a 50-50 balance between horses driven by their own trainers and horses driven by driving specialists, the *catch drivers.* Thirty years ago, the catch driver would be the oddity.

The trend toward catch driving has raised the standards of driving in general. It's inevitable that somebody who specializes in an activity gets better. Does this make the catch driver a better bet? Not necessarily. The trainer/ driver may be better in certain situations:

➤ Trainers do know their horses better than anyone else, even the most sensitive catch driver.

➤ Trainers stand to profit more than any catch driver if the horse wins and may have the stronger motivation.

If the trainer is a competent driver (and some of them are more than competent), he may be the better bet.

Good trainer/drivers are more difficult to identify than good catch drivers. They usually make far fewer starts, so they rarely show up on lists of top dash winners. If they have one or more very successful horses, you may find their names on the lists of top money winners. But they may not be highly placed on the UDR lists or the percentage lists either, even if they are extremely good drivers. Here's why:

➤ They may be more likely than good catch drivers to drive first-time starters.

➤ They may be more likely to drive horses coming off injury layoffs.

➤ They may drive their difficult horses that need seasoning or careful handling.

➤ They can't pick and choose among several stables' horses.

Their statistics may suggest that they are poor drivers rather than the careful trainers that they actually are. More even than catch drivers, trainer/drivers require examination of past performance and results charts to identify the ones who are effective.

Driver's Weight and Age

There's been a long-standing belief in harness racing that the weight of the driver doesn't matter much. Unlike in flat racing, where it's universally accepted that weight slows a horse down, weight in harness racing is somehow believed to be more fluid. It's where the driver places his weight, the believers say, not the weight itself.

The fiction that weight doesn't matter got itself established in the era when everybody was a trainer/driver. Some superb trainers who never met a calorie they didn't like still managed to win with their superbly trained horses. Those trainers would rarely get a mount and would never get a win if they tried to be catch drivers today.

Inside Track

The driver's weight matters most on tracks that are muddy, deep, or otherwise less than fast.

Today's most successful drivers almost never weigh more than 150 pounds, and many of them are below 140. A driver's weight doesn't matter quite so much as a rider's weight does, but we do know for sure that horses pulling lighter weights almost always go faster than those pulling heavier weights, all else being equal. The proof of it is in the program. In a sport where a driver's weight isn't supposed to matter, most tracks print the driver's weight right below the name of the horse.

Conventional harness racing wisdom also has it that the driver's age, like his weight, doesn't much matter. Every now and then, the United States Trotting Association likes to add up the number of octogenarian drivers who have started at least one race during the year. The figure usually stands at about half a dozen. Dozens, possibly even hundreds, of people in their 60s and 70s drive and sometimes win races. Harness racing may be the only significant sport in the world in which elderly people can compete as seriously and as actively as they do. But should you bet on them?

You're told that you may bet on elderly drivers, or young drivers, or middle-aged drivers according to their records, not their ages. At the same time, harness racing is the only one of the racing sports where the age of the two-legged participant is often included right on the program.

Drivers, like other people, can't deny a couple of basic facts. Age brings experience, information, and wisdom, but it takes away reaction time, aerobic capacity, and muscle strength. In harness racing, the ideal balance seems to be somewhere in the 30s and 40s.

Female Drivers

The sulky has been even less hospitable than the racing saddle to women, probably because the weight advantage enjoyed by women doesn't matter in harness racing. On the other hand, Standardbreds are generally less difficult than Thoroughbreds, and upper body strength doesn't matter as much either. The answer to the scarcity of women drivers probably lies in the sport's fascination with tradition. There didn't used to be females in the sulkies, and some people think that's the way it should always be.

When you do come across a female driver, consider her experience level, which probably won't be high, as well as her ranking on the lists we've talked about, which will probably be even lower. The charts, not her sex, will probably mean points against her.

From the Horse's Mouth

The **lines** are the reins that connect drivers' hands to the horse's bit. They are both steering wheel and brakes.

Driving Equipment

Harness racing, which by itself keeps hundreds of horse equipment producers profitable, requires the driver, as well as the horse, to wear and carry extraneous items. Like jockeys, drivers must wear safety helmets. Unlike jockeys, they are required to wear safety vests in many racing jurisdictions. Many drivers don't like the vests, claiming that they're bulky and uncomfortable. With weight of less concern, more rather than fewer tracks are requiring the vests. Neither item of equipment affects the outcome of the race, but they do help assure that you can follow favorite drivers with some confidence that they'll be around next week.

Chapter 8

Courses for Horses

In This Chapter

➤ Track size and shape

➤ Track bias

➤ Off tracks

➤ Turf tracks

➤ Artificial surfaces

North American Thoroughbred tracks, all of which are more or less oval-shaped, range in circumference from the $1/2$ mile of Northampton to the $1^1/2$ miles of Belmont Park, with every gradation of distance in between.

Quarter Horse racing usually takes place on a small oval with a chute that creates at least a full $1/4$-mile straightaway. Many Thoroughbred tracks also use chutes so that all races, whatever their length, finish at the same place.

Harness tracks come in three incarnations. There are a handful of one-mile tracks, most of which share the year with Thoroughbred racing. Most of the rest are either $1/2$-mile or $5/8$-mile ovals.

In both flat and harness racing, the smaller the circumference of the track, the sharper the turns. The more the turn resembles a hairpin, the more likely strategy, accident, and chance will play a part in the result of a race.

Inside Track

A race that begins in a chute often has an unusually long run to the first turn. This takes away much of the advantage of a good start, so habitually poor starters often do well in races that come out of a chute.

Here are some of the problems with sharp turns:

➤ Sharp turns exaggerate the ground lost by horses who race wide.

➤ Sharp turns are difficult for horses who come from behind because it's hard to pass other horses on a turn. Small tracks are almost all turn.

➤ Sharp turns are stressful for equine bones and joints because they force the horse to transfer his weight to his left side to maintain his balance.

➤ Some horses are simply too clumsy to race well on sharp turns. They manage to get their feet tangled and their sense of balance confused.

Harness racing acknowledges the importance of track size by telling you in the past performance charts the circumference of the track where the race occurred. In Thoroughbred racing, track size in previous races is usually not shown in past performance charts, but most past performance publications and some track programs have a chart that lists tracks, often including information on track size.

Inside Track

A small, agile-looking Thoroughbred with an average record on a large track may improve dramatically if he moves to a small, sharp-turned track. His odds may be long, based on his previous performances.

The Biased Racetrack

Every track has a bias. No, that doesn't mean it prefers brown horses to gray ones. It means that it favors certain running styles.

➤ **Rail bias.** If no bias at all is present, the rail (meaning the part of the track closest to the inside rail) is the place to be because it's the shortest way around the track. But the rail is usually the lowest part of the racing surface, making it vulnerable to either hardening or softening, depending on what material the track is made of. The rail position may be good or it may be bad, depending on the individual track bias.

➤ **Position bias.** At some tracks, horses who get to the lead early almost always stay there, unless some far superior horse comes along and catches them. At other tracks, getting an early lead is more like the kiss of death, and even far inferior horses pass early leaders before the finish line. This difference is probably a result of the depth of the loose material on top of the track (more on that later).

You recognize bias by paying attention to the results of previous races. Each day, look at what happened in yesterday's races at the track, trying to pick out patterns. Did every horse that won stay on the rail? Did they come up on the outside? Did early speed hold or did it fold? If you have self-control, watch a few races each day before you bet to see if you can identify any bias for that day.

Deep Tracks

A track with more than 3 inches of *cushion* is deep, and the horses who race on it have to work as their hooves dig through the surface. The more cushion, the more difficult the work. A deep track is a slow one, producing slower times than others.

From the Horse's Mouth

Cushion is the loose material on the surface of the track. It's made of sand, clay, organic materials, or occasionally synthetic fibers, usually in some combination.

Deep tracks also affect race outcomes in the following ways:

➤ A deep track is more tiring to the horses than a harder one, favoring horses with stamina.

➤ Horses can't maintain top speed for long, penalizing front runners.

➤ Horses that like to come from far off the pace suffer because the slowness of the track makes it difficult for them to make up a lot of ground.

➤ Horses with tendon or soft tissue problems often suffer on deep tracks. Avoid a horse with evidence of a bowed tendon on a track with a lot of cushion.

➤ Horses with sore hooves often suffer less because of the reduced concussion that occurs on deep tracks.

Hard Tracks

Hard tracks have problems of their own, and they produce a special dilemma in the minds of track officials. Hard surfaces produce faster race times, which almost every-body likes, but really hard tracks can sometimes be hard on the horses.

In flat racing, few track superintendents nowadays use less than $2^1/_4$ inches of loose material on top of the track surface. Those who lean toward the bottom end of cush-ioning produce tracks that do this:

➤ They often allow early speed to hold on longer than expected, giving an advantage to quick horses who break well.

➤ They create concussion and can be very hard on horses with any kind of hoof or joint soreness. Although they don't cause as much tendon stretch as deeper tracks, hard tracks focus and concentrate pain and are in general much harder on unsound horses.

➤ Tracks with little cushion sometimes have less bias of any kind. There's not enough loose material for dramatic variation in depth from one area of the track to another.

Artificial Surfaces

American racing began a lengthy flirtation with artificial track surfaces in the late 1970s. Engineers developed a variety of petrochemical substances to serve as either the firm base or the loose surface material. Artificial racing surfaces were touted as safer, easier to maintain, and possibly faster. None of these claims proved true, at least to the satisfaction of most flat racing people. Most Thoroughbred racetracks that installed artificial surfaces replaced the fake dirt with the real stuff.

Should you find yourself standing, past performance chart in hand, watching a field of horses march to the post on fake dirt, keep these points in mind:

➤ Artificial surfaces create very opinionated horses. Some horses really love them, and some really hate them. You don't know which it's going to be until the horse races on them.

➤ Betting on a field of horses who've never raced on the track is like betting on a field of first-time starters, except that they probably won't show baby horse antics like trying to run in the wrong direction or biting their lead pony. You pay your money and take your chances.

➤ Artificial surfaces are as prone to bias as any other surface, in spite of the fact that they're supposed to be consistent. Many are noticeably deeper at the rail, which means that horses that like to go wide aren't as disadvantaged as they are on most dirt tracks.

➤ A horse that shows good form in the mud on a dirt
track isn't necessarily going to run well on a wet
artificial surface. Some of the good mud form is due
to a willingness to be hit in the face by slop, which
won't happen in fake dirt.

Harness Track Surfaces

Harness racing requires a much shallower surface than flat
racing because the wheels of the sulky would be bogged
down in loose material of any great depth. The relative
hardness is no problem for harness horses, whose less
stressful gait allows them to remain sound on a track
that would cause gallopers to break down. What's more,
harness racing thrives on fast times. Between the sulky's
requirements and the desire for speed, harness track
superintendents do little experimentation with depth.

Artificial Surfaces

Harness racing has been more hospitable to artificial
surfaces, partially because wintertime racing at major
tracks has become an important part of the sport. Sleet
might cause cancellation at a dirt track, but you can race
(if not enjoy it) on icy artificial tracks. They're also better
in rain because mud and sulky wheels don't mix.

Harness horses don't seem to have the extremes of
attitude toward artificial surfaces as running horses do,
and you usually can make wagering decisions based on
something other than whether it was God or chemical
engineers who made the cushion.

Mud

It's possible to specialize in wet tracks at all levels of
Thoroughbred racing. Some stallions produce a high
percentage of horses that perform well in the mud. Some
trainers are particularly skilled at developing mudders,

and some jockeys know how to get the most out of horses racing over off tracks.

Identifying good wet track horses is not particularly hard. Here's what you look for in a horse that's going to run well on a rainy day:

➤ He has wet track form. Look in his past performances for the symbols *sly, my, hvy;* these symbols describe increasing degrees of wetness in a track. (More on the specifics in Chapter 12.) If he ran well in a race with a symbol, he should be capable of running on a track that isn't dry. The charts sometimes help you by printing an asterisk next to the name of a good mudder, but they miss some and praise others who don't deserve it.

➤ He is bred for wet track racing.

➤ He has big flat feet (go to the saddling enclosure and take a look).

➤ He has early speed, which tends to last longer in the mud. Come-from-behind horses can't get moving as easily, and when they do they find themselves carrying several extra pounds of mud.

➤ He has run well on the turf. Nobody's quite sure why good turf horses are often good mudders, but it may have something to do with those big flat feet.

➤ He doesn't have to be unsound, but if he is, it might not bother him as much as on dry tracks. Mud is softer and less concussive.

Quarter Horses and Standardbreds

Quarter Horses running on wet tracks have the same sense of slipping that Thoroughbreds do, but rain has far less effect on the outcome of the short races. Because Quarter Horses usually run stretched across the track rather than as a parade, one in front of the other, mud kickback isn't a concern. Neither do you have to consider the effect of early speed lasting longer than usual. It's nice to know the horse's previous form on off tracks, but overall past performance is more important.

Harness racing used to be very vulnerable to dramatic form changes in the mud, even though the cushion is shallower and less mud is thrown back to hit the horses in the face and cake on his equipment. The drag of sulky wheels through any amount of mud would cause misery to horse, driver, and bettor, and serious students of wagering on harness racing would often refuse to place a bet on anything but a dry day. That's changed, thanks to synthetic surfaces, better track design for drainage, better sulky design, and the fact that you would miss a lot of good races if you refused to bet on an off track.

Harness horses are also opinionated about mud, some racing well and some racing poorly, but you'll find that the extremes are much closer together than in Thorough-bred racing. Racing on off tracks does affect harness racing in one important way. The final time will be slower, anywhere from one to five seconds slower than it would have been on a dry track. Keep this in mind when you're assessing past performances.

Inside Track

Bettors sometimes don't notice the fact that a slow race or
two in a horse's recent past took place on an off track.
They may dismiss the horse as too slow to bet on. If you're
observant, you may get good odds on a horse that's faster
than he looks.

Track Grooming

You'll see the tractor-pulled harrows on the track between
races, raking and smoothing the surface pitted by the
previous race. You'll also see water trucks depositing
thousands of gallons of water during the racing day.

The better the track, the more thorough the harrowing.
The noisy, lumbering machine might look like a refugee
from a monster truck competition, but it's a welcome
sight to all horsemen. It should be just as welcome to
bettors because it helps assure that the horse you select
will run according to his ability, not according to where
he's lucky enough to place his feet.

Turf Racing

Racing on the grass, usually called *turf,* is a special and
unique category in North American racing. Although it's
the rule rather than the exception in the rest of the world,
here it comprises only a small fraction of all racing. But
grass races make up a disproportionate number of important stakes races, so most major Thoroughbred tracks now
have turf courses in addition to their dirt racing strips.

You won't find cheap claiming races on the turf, and you'll find very few races for sprinters or two-year-olds. American turf racing is mostly for mature, proven horses at middle distances or longer.

As with mud racing, turf racing is better suited for some horses than others. First, look for good past performances in races on the turf. They're identified by a *T* next to the name of the race. Then, consider these qualifications:

➤ Turf sires and grandsires produce turf runners.

➤ The so-called *turf foot* features a wide hoof with a low heel.

➤ Most good turf runners have long strides but high action, meaning that they raise their knees high as they gallop along.

➤ Turf racing usually favors horses who like to come from behind, even at sprint distances.

➤ Imported horses with good records in their native countries usually perform well. The horse will have a two- or three-letter symbol next to his name in the program (*Ire*, *GB*, *Fra*, and so on).

Wet Turf

Turf courses don't produce mud, but they do change when they get wet. On an extremely rainy day, turf racing will be canceled, and the race will be transferred to the main track. Many of the horses will be scratched, but those who remain may show some good performances on muddy main tracks. Examine the past performance charts to identify them. Foreign horses and those who've never run on a dirt track are usually poor bets when a turf race is transferred to the dirt.

If it's only a little damp and the race remains on the turf, the grass will be listed as good, yielding, or soft, depending on how wet it is. Some excellent turf horses despise wet grass, and you can usually pick them by studying their past performances.

Chapter 9

The Long, the Short and the In-Between

In This Chapter

➤ Sprints

➤ Middle-distance races

➤ Routes

➤ The Standardbred Mile

➤ Quarter Horse distances

Because horses vary not only in their speed but in their ability to carry speed over increasing distances, any variation in length matters. That fact can be frustrating to trainers, bettors, and horses alike.

Harness and Quarter Horse racing have dealt with the frustration problem by limiting the variation. Standard-breds race one mile, with a few exceptions that we'll talk about later. Quarter Horses almost always race 440 yards or less, also with a few exceptions.

In Thoroughbred racing, distances vary. Although this variation can be frustrating, it leads to excitement, opportunity, and even a little mystery.

What's Short and What's Not

Because racetracks and turf courses vary in shape and size, races of almost any length are possible. You'll see races identified as being "about 6 ½ furlongs" or "1 mile and 70 yards" or "1 and ⁵/₁₆ mile." No matter how odd the number, all races fit into one of three general categories (shown in the following table), making everyone's decision-making process a little easier.

Race	Distance
Sprint	7 furlongs and under
Middle distance	1 to 1 ¹/₈ miles
Route	1 ³/₁₆ miles and up

From the Horse's Mouth

A **route** is a distance race, not the path a horse takes to get to the finish line.

The Sprinter

Six furlongs is the most common sprint distance, but you'll also see races of 5, 5½ , and 7 furlongs. Early in the year, some tracks schedule ½ mile races for two-year-olds.

It's not clear whether the horses were bred to suit the short races or whether the races were shortened to suit the horses, but it doesn't matter. You'll find yourself paying most of your handicapping attention to the sprint distances.

The following rules of sprint racing apply to all races of less than one mile, but you'll find that their importance is greatest the shorter the race is:

➤ Inside post positions are best, unless there's an anti-rail bias at the track (see Chapter 8).

➤ A good break from the gate is vital. Otherwise, you lose.

➤ Early speed is equally vital, although a horse doesn't have to get an early lead to win.

➤ Contrary to popular opinion, sprints are often won by a horse who comes from behind, but never from far behind. If there are several horses who are likely to produce early speed, a horse who runs off the pace is likely to be the winner.

Inside Track

If the track's configuration causes a very long run to the first turn (a common occurrence in a 7-furlong race), the outside post position is preferable to an inside one for a horse with early speed.

The Middle–Distance Horse

Middle-distance races are usually 1 or 1 $^1/_8$ miles, but you'll also see events of 1 mile 70 yards and 1 $^1/_{16}$ miles. The difficulty of the middle distance is also its glory. It's too long for a *stamina*-free sprinter, but it's too short for a speed-free plodder.

From the Horse's Mouth

Stamina is the kind of endurance a horse needs to win beyond the shortest sprint distances.

As with all races, the proof is in the past performance. Look for your middle-distance winners like this:

➤ If you can't find a true middle-distance specialist (a horse with a good record at the distance), look for a sprinter to stretch out rather than a distance runner to speed up.

➤ Look for a horse with speed to get good early position. A horse can come from behind at the middle distances, but they aren't long enough for a real laggard to get there.

➤ Don't look too much at post position, unless there's an unusually short distance between the starting gate and the first turn. In that case, your horse should be as near as possible to the inside post.

➤ Look at weight, but you rarely have to make it the deciding factor. Figure that five extra pounds will lose the horse $^1/_5$ second, which equals a length.

Middle-distance races constitute only a small percentage of all races in North America, but they make up the majority of stakes events. So if you want to bet on the big ones, learn to identify the good prospects.

The Router

There are few races longer than 1 ¹/₈ miles, but those few include the most prestigious ones. Routes are challenging to everybody.

Because few horses are bred for routes, most modern horses would prefer to be heading back to the barn long before they get to the finish line of a 1 ¹/₂-mile race. Trainers aren't much more enthusiastic, because they are faced with deciding whether to train for the few big races or the many lesser ones. Bettors often don't much like them either because past performance information is usually limited.

But if you want to pick a winner in the Kentucky Derby, the Santa Anita Handicap, or the Breeders' Cup Classic, here are the rules:

➤ Effective routers are often light of body. They can be tall, but not excessively heavy. They usually have modest musculature, but most have deep shoulders and wide chests for lung capacity.

➤ Post position doesn't matter, unless the field is so large that there's a danger of crowding at the first turn.

➤ Early speed isn't vital, but if only one horse in the race has it, he can steal away to a big early lead that nobody else can catch.

➤ Enough speed to stay in contact with the leaders (however fast or slow they are) *is* vital. Routes are almost exclusively for top-class horses, and such a field is rarely going to be caught by a horse who drops much more than a dozen lengths off the pace.

➤ Weight matters a lot. At 1 $\frac{1}{2}$ miles, figure a loss of 2 lengths for every five-pound difference in weight. At 1 $\frac{1}{2}$ miles, it's more like 3 lengths.

The Two-Turn Enigma

Some races are longer than others of the same length. Really. It's a result of the two-turn enigma.

Horses who compete in a one-mile race over a track that's a mile in circumference will go around two turns. A mile race on a 1 $\frac{1}{2}$-mile track will need only one turn. A horse that can win a one-turn mile may not have enough stamina for a two-turn mile. Even a horse that wins a one-turn 1 $\frac{1}{8}$-mile race may not have enough for a two-turn mile.

Actually, it's probably not such an enigma, because running around a turn requires more energy than running straight. But the problem exists, and if you're looking at a past performance chart that tells you that a horse won at a mile or 1 $\frac{1}{8}$ mile race at Belmont Park, don't assume that he can run that distance at Churchill Downs or any other mile track. Until he's raced around two turns, he's still a sprinter.

Standardbred Racing

Despite its origins in a sport that featured competitions over distances as long as 50 miles, modern harness racing confines itself to short, uniform events. The races are normally one mile, and that fact means that you rarely have to consider distance in your handicapping equation. But rarely doesn't mean never.

Odd Distances

You'll occasionally come across races that aren't exactly one mile in length. They may be a fraction over or under one mile, usually because they have to accommodate a track whose size or circumference doesn't quite allow a mile race to finish at the wire.

If the variation from a mile is minor (it's usually just a few yards), you can analyze the race as if it were the standard distance. Just remember in studying past performance charts that fractional times will be different on these tracks. Use the track variant table published in almost all programs and past performance publications.

The race that's nowhere near a mile is very rare, at least in North America. They're sometimes shorter than normal, perhaps ¾ mile, or they may be longer, either a 1 ¼ or a 1 ½. These distances are generally added to a race card as an experiment to generate interest.

Inside Track

You'll occasionally find a horse that benefits from extra or fewer yards. Look for one who's usually caught at the wire or who can't get to the front until a couple of strides past the finish.

If you're faced with a nonstandard race and want to bet on it, look for the obvious. In the short ones, try to identify horses that always leave well. In the longer races, look for horses that are in the habit of finishing strongly. There's no guarantee that they can carry that strength beyond a mile, but there is an absolute guarantee that a horse struggling at the end of a mile won't get a sudden burst of renewed energy from additional yardage.

Heat Racing

There's one other situation where total distance varies: heat racing. This vestige of old-time racing is fast disappearing. When the sport's most famous event, the Hambletonian, shrank from heats to a single dash in 1997, the death knell for heat racing may have been rung. But the corpse still has a little life in it, and some events, including a few major stakes, are still determined by heats.

In heat racing, a horse usually has to win two separate dashes to win the event. All horses compete in dash one and dash two. If the winner of dash one also wins dash two, he wins the event. If another horse wins dash two, they race off in dash three. Sometimes all horses race in three preliminary dashes, and sometimes the first dash is split.

Obviously, a horse needs endurance to race two or more miles on the same day, even though the miles have a little time between them. If you're trying to pick winners in heat races, do it like this:

➤ Assess the first heat as if it were any other dash, according to past performance, appearance of health and soundness, driver, trainer, and any other statistics you choose.

➤ Assess subsequent heats according to performance in the first heat.

➤ Pay extra attention to appearance during the post parade in any heats after the first. Try to identify signs of exhaustion, such as sweating or reluctance to move out. Sometimes a horse will even manage to look a little thinner than he did in the first dash.

➤ Remember that order of finish in the first dash usually determines post position in the second. The winner is on the rail, the second place horse next out, and so on. This position gives the first winner an automatic advantage at most tracks, particularly small ones.

➤ Check past performances for horses that always finish well. This might demonstrate stamina for heat racing.

➤ Look at how recently and how often the horse has raced. You want to see that the horse started within two weeks of the current event, but you don't want to see that he's started every week for two months. He's bound to be exhausted.

➤ Or just skip the bet and enjoy the race. Nowadays, only the best horses race in heats, and a good horse is always a joy to watch.

Quarter Horses

The standard length of a Quarter Horse race is 440 yards, although there are events ranging down to 220 yards for very young horses. In recent years, the sport has added races of 660, 770, and 870 yards, but they're rare.

All but the two longest Quarter Horse races require neither strategy nor pacing because every horse runs as fast as he can for every step. Look for the soundest, most consistent, best-conditioned horse you can find without consideration for distance.

The 770s and 870s usually aren't won by the same horses who excel in the shorter races. Keep these points in mind in the distance events:

➤ Thoroughbred blood is useful. If the sire or dam is Thoroughbred, you'll see the letters *TB* next to its name. Unless you keep up with breeding, you won't be able to spot Thoroughbred blood any further back in the pedigree.

➤ A horse should show evidence of running very strongly at the end of the shorter races. He shouldn't be in the habit of being caught at the wire at a quarter mile.

➤ A horse should have an inside post position because the long races are run around turns.

➤ If you've seen the horses run before, look for one with a longer stride than the average racing Quarter Horse.

➤ Good starts are very important, but they're not quite everything as they are in the short events.

Chapter 10

Keeping It Competitive

In This Chapter

- ➤ Claiming races
- ➤ Allowance races
- ➤ Stakes races
- ➤ Weight assignments
- ➤ Standardbred races

Racing secretaries design races of all kinds: races for good horses and bad ones, inexperienced horses and old campaigners, and male horses and females. Add to the mix the varying quality of racetracks, and you get races for horses of all kinds and talents.

But if every horse entered exactly the race it belonged in, the best of a bad bunch would almost always win, as would the best of a good bunch. There would be no excitement and very little betting revenue.

So racing secretaries add some qualifications to each race to make it harder for everyone—things such as weight breaks for some horses make it harder for others, extra entry fees for stake races make it more expensive to take a shot at big money, and claiming makes it risky for everybody. Finding the best race that a horse can win is the challenge for the horse's connections, and finding the best horse that can win a race is the challenge for the rest of us.

Claiming Races

The majority of flat races and a substantial percentage of harness races in North America are claiming races, in which every horse is available for purchase at a specified price. On any day's race card, you're likely to see claimers in all but one or two races. Because of their dominance, you must understand the principles of claiming races if you plan to bet on or even enjoy today's racing.

Even though all the horses are for sale, not everybody can buy them. Rules vary from track to track, but usually only people who train or own at least one other horse at the track can drop a claim into the box. This qualification matters to all of us because owners and trainers receive at least a minimal background check before they are licensed. The license is no guarantee of honesty, but it does assure that they've never done time at a penitentiary for race fixing and fraud.

The claims are dropped into the claiming box before the starting gate opens. The successful claimant (more than one claim results in drawing lots) owns the horse as soon as the race starts, win, lose, or dead. This means that casual claims are usually not made.

Are All Claimers Cheap Horses?

No. Claiming prices are determined for each race by the racing secretary to approximate the value of the horses he hopes to attract to the race. Their value is, understandably, based on their racing ability. The price may range from $1,200 for the worst horses at a small track to $50,000 for the best claimers at a big track. Secretaries sometimes experiment with high-price claiming races (upwards of $100,000), but these are rare.

Price matters to the bettor because the price the owner is willing to take for the horse is a good indication of his quality. A high price means the horse is sound and probably consistent. A low price, especially at small tracks, means the horse has serious problems. An extremely low-priced claimer who used to race at a higher level is probably very unsound. He's also in possession of an owner who should do the right thing and retire him.

In Standardbred racing, where there's no weight assigned, racing secretaries use price almost exclusively to lure intriguing horses, especially better ones, to claiming races. The secretary will allow a 25 percent increase in claiming price for female horses and maybe 25 percent for three-year-olds, so a four-year-old gelding can be claimed for $10,000, but the three-year-old filly racing next to him will cost $15,000. The fans will probably see a better-quality filly whose trainer wouldn't risk losing her for $10,000, but might for $15,000.

Conditioned Races

In Standardbred racing, you'll see conditioned races in which the horses aren't necessarily subject to claiming. They often feature horses on par in talent with claimers, and you'll notice that their past performance lines may show starts in both other conditioned races and claiming races.

THE MEADOWLANDS
SIXTH RACE
PURSE $15,000

ONE MILE TROT
WEDNESDAY FEBRUARY 18, 1998

EXACTA AND TRIFECTA WAGERING; RACING PICK 3 (RACES 6-8)

FILLIES & MARES N/W $15500 IN LAST 5 STARTS; STAKE EARNINGS EXCLUDED
AE: N/W $50000 LIFETIME

WARM UP COLOR—YELLOW

PLEASE ASK FOR HORSE BY PROGRAM NUMBER

PROGRAM NUMBER	Date	Trk	Purse	Cond Temp	Class	Dis	Leader's Time 1/4 1/2 3/4	Winner's Time PP	1/4	1/2	3/4	Str	Fin	Ind¼ Time	Ind Time	Odds	Driver	Med	Comment	Order of Finish First Second Third

Red · Driver—WILLIAM FAHY Brown-Orange 170 (167-8-8-21-.116) · Trainer—Brett Bittle (14-1-1-4-.206) · Breeder-Jerome W Cassata

1 ANNA STELLA
b f 4 by Royal Prestige-Hooker Lure-Bonefish · Tom Crouch, Lexington, Ky.

2-11	¹M1		15000	ft 45	FMnw15000	1	29¹	57⁴ 127	156² 4	57²	55²	63³⁰	5³	5⁹⅛	30¹	158¹	9-1	JoCampbl		no threat	EmrdSStr.Anah.WndBkMyWngs-6
2-5	³M1		18000	sy 34	nw10000L6	1	29⁴	59¹ 129¹	158² 6	99³⁰	85²⁰	89²⁰	4⁵¾	3⁴	283	159¹	6-1	JoCampbl		bad cover	Spdy2mnt.MglMntsr.AnaStla-10
1-23	³M1		35000	sy 35	D-nw4Lc	1	29⁴	58² 129⁵	157 1	41⁸	33³	x8²¹¹	7⁰⁵	7³²½	303	203²	11-1	JoCampbl		on move broke	GvsCsr.VctryIsMn.GtBrodChck-9
1-16	⁰⁹M1		15000	ft 30	nw4Lc	1	30	100² 129¹	158² 6	55⁹	55²	5¹⁰⅓	6¹¹⅛	6¹⁴⅛	30	201¹	9-2	CManzi		jammed strtch	HisHghwy.DmdsRnwy.GtBodchk-8
1-9	⁷M1		15000	ft 48	nw4Lc	1	29	58 128¹	157⁴ 5	8¹¹	10¹¹⅛	10¹⁰⅓	79³	25²⅛	284	158¹	21-1	CManzi		flying late	GvsCaesar.AnaStla.JazB-10

12-1 · Lifetime 1998 5 0 1 1 $6,660 · 1997 13 4 2 1 $76,131 1:57³ M1Q · Lifetime $82,791 3, 1:57³ 1Q

Blue · Driver—MIKE LACHANCE Red-Black-White 155 (338-59-42-40-.283) · Trainer—Joseph King (8-1-3-0-.333) · Breeder-Oakbrook Stable

2 VICTORY IS MINE
b f 4 by Valley Victory-Armbro Jilly-Speedy Crown · Lindy Farms of Conn, Paul & Antoinette M.Nigito, Conn, N.J.

2-6	¹¹Fhld		13500	ft 46	OPENHC	1	28³	58³ 128	157⁶ 6x	x8⁰⁵	8	8⁰⁵	8⁰⁵	8⁰⁵	301	158¹	5-2	GBrennan			MacActon.Amah.PrmrtKsd-8
1-23	³M1		35000	sy 35	D-nw4Lc	1	29²	58² 128³	157 5	21	21½	21¼	2¼	2⁵¾	281	157	6-1	CManzi		winner 2 tuff	GvsScr.VctryIsMn.GtBodchck-9
1-16	⁹M1		15000	ft 30	nw4Lc	1	29²	100² 131¹	159³ 1	1¹¹	21¼	21¼	1¹½	25⅛	291	200⁴	9-5	CManzi		winner 2 tuff	GvsCaesar.VictoryIsMn.Astrod-8
1-9	³M1		15000	ft 48	nw4Lc	1	29	58¹ 128¹	157⁴ 6	1¹	1¹½	11½	2⁴	2ᴺᴷ	292	157⁴	5-1	MLachanc		well driven	VctryIsMn.Crs1m.Ohcm1rkt-9
6-1	⁷V		15000		QUA	1	29⁴	58² 128¹	159¹ 1	2²	23	2⁴	23	2ᴺᴷ	294	159⁴		NBLachanc			TsrAlwys.VctryIsMn.KysnCln-4

6-1V · Lifetime 1998 16 4 0 5 $20,000 1:57⁴ M1 · 1997 16 4 0 5 $141,040 1:55² Lex1 · Lifetime $165,090 3, 1:55³ 1

White · Driver—CATELLO MANZI White-Lt Blue-Blue 175 (247-31-24-25-.132) · Trainer—Donna Marshall (21-5-3-0-.317) · Breeder-Seester Farms Inc.

3 EMERALD SEELSTER
b f 4 by Cheyenne Spur-Edbars Nanci-Speedy Rodney · Martin J.O'Hare,Phoenixville,Pa.

2-11	⁴M1		15000	ft 45	FMnw15000	1	29¹	57⁴ 127	156² 1	11½	11½	11½	12½	156²	292	156²	5-2	CManzi		hr-d safe	EmrdSStr.Anah.WndBkMyWngs-6
2-5	³M1		18000	gd 34	nw10000L6	1	29¹	59¹ 129¹	158¹ 4	64½	64⅜	63²	2ᴺᴷ	2ᴺᴷ	274	157¹	7-1	RPierce		closed inside	SmkyLgnd.EmrdSStr.WhrdWd-9
2-1	⁷M1		50000	ft 32	D-nw2Lc	1	28²	58² 127⁴	157² 6	44	21¹⁰	16	1½	12½	293	157²	*5-2	RPierce		well driven	EmrdSStr.YkBrodo.KysLaNa-10
1-21	⁹M1		12500	ft 30	nw2Lc	1	28³	58² 129	158⁴ 5	11½	11½	12	11½	1¹½	294	158⁴	7-5	JMarshal		much the best	E-rradSStr.SwsOn.IcastK-11
1-7	³M1		12500	sy 40	nw2Lc	1	30¹	101 101	130³ 159⁴ 2	3⁴	2¹³⁰	1ⁿᴰ	1¹½	1¹½	29	159⁴	4-5	JMarshal		handy sort	EmrdSStr.WitsBka.OhBoStr-8

2-1 · Lifetime 1998 5 4 1 0 $49,500 1:56² M1 · 1997 20 2 4 2 $65,769 1:58² GSP1 · Lifetime $115,269 4, 1:56² 1

Here's a typical set of conditions in a Standardbred race.

Conditioned races have qualifications for entry. The race may be open only to horses that haven't won $1,000 in their last five starts, horses that have never won anything, horses that haven't won as a three-year-old, or horses that *have* won in the past few months.

Bad Bet

Never skip reading the conditions and qualifications at the top of the program page before every race. You may find a phrase that allows in a top horse against weak competition.

Allowance Races

These Thoroughbred and Quarter Horse events usually attract better horses than claiming races because the horse is not for sale. But they feature varying levels of competition, just like claiming races, and trainers still have to try to find the best race while bettors try to find the best horse.

Allowance races are similar to harness racing's conditioned events because they usually limit entry to horses who haven't won a certain number of races in a certain length of time. But racing secretaries can design allowance races for almost any horse they want to see entered. A race for horses that haven't won a race in 1999 might seem like one for pretty feeble animals, but it could allow in the millionaire Kentucky Derby winner of 1998. Always read those conditions.

Quinella, Exacta & Trifecta Wagering
1st Leg Pick 3
Freedom Village

Purse $9,700

6th

Allowance

(INCLUDES $2,000 FOA). FOUR YEAR OLDS AND UPWARD WHICH HAVE NOT WON TWO RACES OTHER THAN MAIDEN, CLAIMING, OR STARTER SINCE OCTOBER 17, 1997 Weight 122 lbs. Non-winners of two races since November 17 allowed, 3 lbs. A race since November 17, 6 lbs. (Races where entered for $12,500 or less not considered in weight allowances).

5 Furlongs

119

Track Record: Arion Fair (4), 116 lbs; :57.1 (03-20-82)

1 **8-1** **GO KAZ** (L)
Ch.g. '93 Sensational Luck-Philip's Nannie by Sir Woodley
Breeder: S & K Stables (OH) (March 31, 1993)
Red, Blue "LL" on White Star

Red

Owner: Miguel Feliciano & Leonard Longo
Trainer: Miguel Feliciano

Benny Feliciano

	1st	2nd	3rd	
1998:	1	1	2	0	$5,040
1997:	11	2	1		$30,980
Life:	28	6	5	4	$67,344

Turf: 1 0 0 0 $700
Off Track: 2 1 0 0 $1,294

Date													Comment	
01Jan98	6Tam	6f	ft	:22⁴⁰	:45⁹⁰	1:11⁴⁰	4↑ Alw10400nw1/x	5	4	2ʰᵈ	1ʰᵈ	1¹⁄₂	1³ Feliciano,B	bfL 116	10.10	81 GKz³, OrMtthew¹, ThndmgStorm ʰᵈ	long drive, prevailed 8
08Nov97	4Tdn	1	wf	:47⁴⁰	1:12⁹⁰	1:38³⁶	3↑ Alw12000nw2/x	5	2¹	2¹⁄₂	2ʰᵈ	2¹⁄₂	3³ Feliciano,B	bfBL116	2.40	84 JysMne3, AlgbrHndrson ⁿˢ, GKz1	drew even, outfinished 6
26Oct97	12Tdn	1	ft	:48⁹⁶	1:13⁴⁰	1:39⁴⁶	3↑ [S]Alw19800cnd	7	1¹	1¹	1¹⁄₂	2¹	2¹¹⁄₂ Feliciano,B	bfBL116	28.00	81 PtsanlAlair 1¹⁄₂, GKz 2¹⁄₂, JJ.Hny 1¹⁄₂	set pace, second best 8
13Oct97	9Tdn	6f	ft	:22²⁰	:45¹⁸	1:11⁰⁴	3↑ [S]OhioSprnt-50k	12	3	6⁴¹⁄₂	5⁴	7⁷¹⁄₂	8⁸¹⁄₄ Felix,J	bfBL122	24.90ᵉ	78 BuckCreek 3, GrapeJuice 1¹⁄₂, InandOver 3	faded 14
21Sep97	12Beu	6f	ft	:22³⁰	:45⁷⁶	1:10⁴⁵	3↑ [S]HoneyJayH-30k	5	7	6⁴	12¹²	12¹⁶¹⁄₂	12²⁶¹⁄₂ Murphy,C	bfBL114	64.10	55 Dnzcode 5, InndOver ¹⁄₂, AncientSecret ⁿᵏ	failed to menace 13
03Aug97	11Tdn	6f	ft	:22⁷⁰	:45⁴⁴	1:11⁰⁰	3↑ Alw14000nw1$/x	6	1	4²¹⁄₂	6³³	5⁵	5⁶¹⁄₂ Feliciano,B	bfBL116	8.00	77 RryOpince 1³, DncLgcy 2, OptimmMde 1	lacked late response 7
03Aug97	11Tdn	1	ft	:49⁹⁶	1:12⁸⁴	1:39⁵⁰	3↑ Alw14000nw2/rfx	3	1¹	1ʰᵈ	1ʰᵈ	1ʰᵈ	2ⁿᵏ Feliciano,B	bfBL116	7.20	82 CMMaria ⁿᵏ, GKz ¹⁄₂, Nstiah'sFlet ⁿᵏ	outfinished, gamely 6
20Jul97	11RD	1¹⁄₁₆	⊗ fm	:48⁹⁰	1:12⁴⁰	1:43⁴⁰	3↑ [S]Buckeye Na-35k	6	2¹¹⁄₂	2ʰᵈ	2ʰᵈ	7⁶¹⁄₂	7⁶¹⁄₂ Trollo,W	bfBL113	20.70	71 Dnzcode ʰᵈ, TsAndy'sTm 4, Rchrd'sRb 1¹⁄₂	pressed pace, gave way 12
22Jun97	4Tdn	1	ft	:47⁴ˣ	1:12¹⁶	1:37⁷⁶	3↑ Alw14000nw2/rfx	5	3	1¹	1¹⁄₂	2ʰᵈ	4²¹⁄₂ Feliciano,B	bfBL122	14.50	79 BckCreek 3, ImprialPas 3, RyalOpulence 1	dueled, tired 8
28May97	6Tdn	1	ft	:48⁴ˣ	1:12⁹²	1:40¹⁰	3↑ Alw13000nw1/rfx	5	1¹⁄₂	1²	1ʰᵈ	1ʰᵈ	1ⁿᵏ Feliciano,B	bfBL116	4.20	79 GoKaz ⁿᵏ, DuNorth ⁿˢ, OutforGold 1³	long drive, all out 7

Workouts: 15Jan98 3f ft :36.00 b   23Dec Tam 4f ft :50.20 b   15Dec Tam 4f ft :50.40 b   05Dec Tam 3f ft :37.80 b

Here's a typical set of conditions for an allowance race.

The word *allowance* in allowance races means a break
in the weights. A non-winner since July might get a
reduction of three pounds; a non-winner all year may
get five. I'll have more on what weight breaks mean later,
but note now that the reductions, as well as conditions,
give trainers and bettors a chance to shop for the most
lucrative potential race for a particular horse.

Maiden Specials

In flat racing, maiden specials are scheduled for horses,
usually two-year-olds, who've never won a race but are
too valuable to be entered for claiming prices. Unlike
maiden claiming races, which usually feature the worst
horses around, maiden specials may include potential
champions. The joy of maiden special is the possibil-
ity that you may see one of the great ones. The agony is
that they are remarkably difficult to figure out.

Many serious bettors avoid maiden specials, without
exception. Others look for signs of life in breeding, workouts, appearances, and connections and bet accordingly.
Some of us prefer to watch and hope.

Stakes Races

Stakes races represent the pinnacle of the sport, whether
it's flat, harness, or steeplechase racing. Stakes races are
always the most lucrative that the track offers, and the
purses are increased by the addition of entry fees paid by
the owners.

It's more complicated, as well as more expensive, to enter
a horse in a stakes race than in other kinds of races, so
you'll often find horses that belong in big races simply
not there. Some races require modest eligibility payments
by owners months or even years in advance. Most will
allow horses not originally made eligible to be entered late
by paying a stiff fee, but some still do not.

Handicap Races

In Thoroughbred racing, many stakes and some allowance races are handicaps, although there are fewer of them than there used to be. In handicap races, the racing secretary or an assistant assigns weight to each horse to try to even them up. The goal is to have every horse finish in a dead heat for first.

A handicap is a challenge to assign, particularly nowadays with quick and easy transportation to other racetracks. Racing secretaries walk a fine line. If handicapping is done right, the best horse will receive so much weight that his trainer will probably take him elsewhere, and the worst horse will carry so little that his trainer will have trouble finding a jockey who can make the weight.

Most handicaps aren't done well, and the race isn't going to come out anywhere near even. But there will be some variation in weight between the entries, and you will have to try to figure out what difference it might make in the outcome.

Weight Watching at the Racetrack

Weight has no official role in Standardbred racing, and it doesn't make a lot of difference in Quarter Horse racing, but it's important—sometimes the deciding factor—in Thoroughbred racing.

In non-handicap events, weights are usually assigned according to the standard scale used in North America. The Jockey Club's Scale of Weights, also known as the weight-for-age scale, is the bible of weight assignments. It's a massive chart, with recommended weights for horses of varying age and sex, racing at each possible distance, and with weights ranging from the 96 pounds to be assigned a three-year-old racing two miles in January to the 130 to be carried by an older horse going a $1/2$ mile in December.

In the real world of racing, no three-year-old is ever going to race two miles in January, and conditions would assure that few horses will carry 130 pounds in any race at any time of the year, but the scale has some basic principles:

➤ Weight assignments go up as distance goes down, for horses of both sexes and all ages.

➤ Weights go up as the season wears down because the horses are supposed to be in better condition later in the year. Actually, many horses are never again as sound and fast as they are in the early spring.

➤ Female horses carry less than male horses. Two-year-old fillies carry three pounds less. Three-year-olds and up carry five pounds less until September, when they carry three pounds less (mares rarely come into heat in the fall and tend to be more competitive then).

The top weight in the average race at the average racetrack will probably be about 122 pounds, with conditions and allowances bringing the weight down for most of the horses entered. The weight each horse is to carry is always printed prominently in the program or past performance publication.

Why It Matters

Horses can carry a lot of weight, even at a gallop. Cow ponies, most of whom are considerably smaller than Thoroughbreds, can dash around under riders who weigh at least 50 pounds more than the heaviest jockey.

What horses can't do under a lot of weight is run as fast as they might otherwise. How much slower they run under how much more weight is the question. Unfortunately, there's no easy answer.

Here are some guidelines, subject to disagreement and variation from track to track. Remember that ¹/₅ second equals a length. Here's what extra weight means at the finish line:

➤ At a sprint distance, a horse will lose ¹/₅ second for every five pounds extra he carries.

➤ At a middle distance, he loses ¹/₅ second for every three to four extra pounds.

➤ At a route distance, he loses ¹/₅ second for every two to three extra pounds.

➤ The heavier the weight, the more speed he loses, whatever the distance. If he's carrying 110 pounds, he probably isn't going to be much slower than the horse carrying 105, all else being equal. But at 125, he may be several lengths slower than the horse carrying 120 that is in all other ways his equal.

Some bettors are thrilled to see a horse assigned a lighter weight than he carried in his last start. They figure he'll be equally thrilled, running much faster with the joy of a reduced burden.

In fact, horses usually receive lighter weight assignments because they haven't been accomplishing anything. A horse that's been performing well recently should pick up a few pounds, not shed them. There's one exception: A horse that's been racing under high imposts in handicaps will greatly appreciate the lighter weight of a scale weight event. He may move up dramatically.

Steeplechase

Racing over fences is sometimes a betting sport, but it's often not. Major tracks such as Belmont, Saratoga, and Keeneland schedule occasional steeplechases as part of the regular racing calendar. These are betting races, with wagering accepted just like any other.

If you're hoping to pick steeplechase winners, whether there's money or pride on the line, follow these rules:

➤ A steeplechase is always a route race, so follow the route rules in Chapter 9.

➤ A good record on the flat is admirable, but success at sprints is no more useful than no experience at all. Look for flat race appearances in middle distances and routes to judge potential.

➤ Past performances in steeplechases are significant, but you're looking for consistency first. Avoid horses that fall. Unless they finish the race, they can't win, no matter how much speed and stamina they have.

➤ Post position and early speed don't matter, unless the first jump is close to the starting gate and the horse has only a short space to get into a good spot to take off.

➤ Behavior does matter because steeplechasers have a great deal of opportunity to bolt, stop, dump their riders, and otherwise destroy their chances. Horses are essentially out of control as they take off and descend from a jump, and any horse who wants to misbehave can opt out of the race at every obstacle.

Qualifiers and Training Races

All Standardbreds take part in non-betting races at some point in their careers. They are required to compete in qualifiers, proving that they are sensible and at least modestly fast, before they're eligible to race with fans' money on them.

Some qualifiers are held at training tracks, and some are held at the regular racetrack. You can't bet on them, but you can usually watch. Don't try to pick winners, but do pay close attention. Whether you attend or just review the qualifier in past performance charts, you'll find a horse's performance to be instructive. Just remember that a qualifier is not quite the same thing as a race. Keep these differences in mind:

➤ Qualifiers are usually slower than a betting race with the same horses would be. There's no money on the line, and the last thing the trainers want is pressure on the horse. He might break stride and fail to qualify.

➤ The trainer probably drove his own horse, and he might not be as talented at driving as the catch driver he'll hire for the actual race.

➤ Unless you were there or recognize the names of the other horses, you won't know the level of the competition. You may see that a horse won a qualifier by 10 lengths, but you won't know if he beat Mr. Ed or a future Niatross.

➤ Some trainers don't want more than an adequate performance by their horses in qualifiers. They want to be able to surprise the competition (and maybe cash a good bet) when real money is on the line.

Chapter 11

How to Place a Bet

In This Chapter

➤ How pari-mutuel betting works

➤ Odds and payoffs

➤ How to place a bet

➤ Straight bets and exotics

➤ Wheeling and boxing

At its most basic, the pari-mutuel system is simple. Every bettor who wants to participate in a race picks the horse he thinks will win. The money paid by all of the bettors is pooled. When the race is over, the pooled money is divided up evenly among everyone who bought a ticket on the winning horse. It makes no difference to the track, which operates the pool, which horse wins. It isn't their money that's paid out; it's the money of the people who hold the losing tickets.

Although the winners each get a share, they don't get exactly the same amount. First, all winners are repaid for their initial investment. The person who bet $2 gets $2 back. A $50 bettor gets back $50. This money is the *return* on the bet. The remainder of the pool is then divided among the winners according to units of $2. The $2 bettor has 1 unit; the $50 bettor has 25 units.

The *profit* on the bet is figured by dividing the number of units possessed by all the bettors into the pool that remains after the return, and then distributing it to the bettors according to the number of units each owns.

Let's pause now for a little arithmetic (proving that the required four years of math in high school really was worthwhile). Follow the steps in this example, or just leap to the conclusion.

➤ Total pool of an imagined race: $450

➤ Two people bet $50 each on the winner (each has 25 $2 units)

➤ Twenty-seven people bet $2 each on the winner (each has one $2 unit)

➤ Return to bettors on their initial investments: $154

➤ Profit due to winning bettors: $296

➤ Units outstanding: 77

➤ Each unit is worth $296 divided by 77, which equals $3.84

➤ The winning $50 bettors each receive $146 ($96 profit plus their $50)

➤ The $2 bettors each receive $5.84 ($3.84 profit plus their $2)

➤ Totals: $146 multiplied by 2 is $292; $5.84 multiplied by 27 is $157.68

➤ Returned to winning bettors: $292 plus $157.68, which is $449.68

Now, having used all that remembered math, here's some bad news: That's not really what you get back.

Takeouts and Breakage

There's *takeout* and *breakage* in each race, and this doesn't mean that a losing bettor had a temper tantrum in a nearby Chinese restaurant. What it means is that less than 100 percent of the entire pool is divided up among the holders of the winning tickets.

The track withholds between 14 and 18 percent of the pool before distribution as the combined profit of the state and the racetrack. The figure varies, depending on how much the state wants. That's takeout. Breakage is the policy of rounding off payoffs to the next lowest dime. Often this money is used to pay off bettors in a *minus pool,* but sometimes it's added to the overall profit.

From the Horse's Mouth

A **minus pool** is one in which there's not enough money to pay back everybody who bet on a horse, plus the track's minimum profit of 10 cents on the dollar. It can occur when an outstanding horse is heavily bet and wins as expected.

The track's percentage goes to pay its operating expenses, including salaries, plant maintenance, and purse money. Both bettors and tracks wish state legislatures would be a little less greedy in demanding their cut, but they've had little luck in convincing politicians to reduce what is in effect a tax on gambling so racing's takeout remains higher than in most forms of gambling.

A separate pool is maintained for each kind of bet in each race. For example, if you're betting to win, your money is combined with that of everybody else who's betting to win and not those who are betting to place or show. In these days of high-speed, high-capacity computers, a remarkable number of pools can be maintained for bets on the same race.

Odds Are, You'll Be Confused

Every track calculates odds for each horse based on the amount of money currently in the pool. Once the race has started and betting is closed, the track figures the final odds on which the payoffs to the winners will be based.

By tradition, payoff figures are based on a $2 bet, even though odds are worked out based on $1. The reason for this is that $2 used to be the minimum bet. Tradition survives, even though most tracks now permit bets of any amount from $1 on up. Once you know the payoff for $2, you can figure what you'll get for any other amount.

> ➤ For $2, divide the amount by 2.

> ➤ For $5, multiply by 2 $1/2$.

> ➤ For $10, multiply by 5.

> ➤ Et cetera.

As for the payoffs you'll get for a win at various odds, here's the simplest way to figure them. First, make sure the odds are based on 1. Change odds of 5 to 2, for example, to 2 $1/2$ to 1. Then multiply the first number by 2. Add your initial $2 investment to the total, and you have your payoff for a $2 bet, $7.

The formula isn't entirely accurate at very short odds because, among other things, there's a minimum profit that you'll get even if everybody holds a winning ticket and there's no losers' money to spread around. But you'll find it works just fine for most horses in most races. If you don't want to do the math, the following table shows a selection of payoffs on a $2 bet for various odds.

Odds	Payoff
1 to 9	$2.20
1 to 5	$2.20
2 to 5	$2.80
1 to 2	$3.00
Even (1 to 1)	$4.00
7 to 5	$4.80
2 to 1	$6.00
5 to 2	$7.00
3 to 1	$8.00
7 to 2	$9.00
4 to 1	$10.00
5 to 1	$12.00
6 to 1	$14.00
7 to 1	$16.00
8 to 1	$18.00
9 to 1	$20.00
10 to 1	$22.00
15 to 1	$32.00

continues

Odds	Payoff
20 to 1	$42.00
50 to 1	$102.00
99 to 1	$200.00

The Tote

For most racegoers, the *tote board* is the map that directs you in and out of the labyrinth of the racing game. The name comes from the Totalisator Company, which used to operate most of the computerized betting systems in North America. Today, other companies operate systems and boards, but the behemoth of the infield is still known as the tote board. Depending on how much money the track is willing to spend on the board and the computer system, the tote can display a lot of information or hardly any.

The bare minimum of information shown would include the following:

➤ Time of day.

➤ Post time to the next race.

➤ Approximate odds of each horse in the next race (you'll see program numbers rather than names).

➤ Results and payoffs of the last race. These are removed as betting progresses on the next race, so nobody is confused. The win, place, show, and fourth-place positions are then used to show the changing order during the next race.

A mid-range board will add this information:

➤ Dollar amounts of pools for win, place, and show

➤ Fractional and final times of the last race (this disappears as betting progresses)

➤ Fractional and final times of the current race

➤ Track condition

➤ Scratches

➤ Inquiry sign

Top-of-the-line totes will add this information:

➤ Weather

➤ Equipment or jockey changes

➤ Mud caulks

➤ Potential payoff for win bet

➤ Pools or potential payoff for exotic bets

➤ Any other information the track deems important

When a track has limited tote space, information other than betting figures will be given over the public address system. You have to both listen and remember to take advantage of it. The tote is much more convenient, and serious racegoers believe that there's no such thing as too much on the tote.

The information on the tote board is tied directly to the computers that keep track of the money bet. The figures are constantly changing, but they do lag behind reality. You won't know the true size of the pools and the actual starting odds until the race is over.

Bad Bet

Although it's useful to pay attention to the pool, the odds, and any money that comes in late (late money is supposed to be smart money, which is money from knowledgeable people), cutting it too late can get you cut out of betting. Because of simulcasting, most betting facilities close the windows precisely at the scheduled post time.

How to Place a Bet

Today, racing offers bettors convenience beyond what even the most customer-friendly bookie could dream of. Tickets no longer have to be preprinted in set amounts, so you can go to any window and put down any amount of money you choose, within reason. No odd-change bets are allowed.

Whether you're a purist or an aficionado of exotics, the process of betting is the same. Racetracks, simulcast facilities, and off-track betting outlets will have a sign near the betting windows telling you how to announce your bet to the pari-mutuel clerk. If you get the required items a little mixed up, the clerk isn't going to refuse your bet. He or she will help you work out the wager you want. The closer you get to the correct order, the quicker you'll have your ticket in hand, and the happier you'll make the people standing in line behind you.

Have your money in hand as you ask for the ticket. You will be expected to give the following information in the following order:

> The name of the racetrack, provided that the windows take bets from more than one racetrack. Otherwise, the present track will be assumed.

> The number of the race.

> The amount of money you want to bet.

> The kind of bet.

> The number (not the name) of the horse.

Inside Track

Speed matters. If you (and the other people in line) don't get your bets in before post time, you'll find yourself shut out. Just don't ask for your ticket so fast that you get the numbers wrong.

Don't get nervous if you can't remember the numbers. Clerks have copies of the program, and most of them will work out what race and what horse you mean.

You may also write down the details of any other bet that you find too intricate to remember. In fact, it's a good idea to write down details if you're combining several complicated bets in one visit to the window.

After you've successfully announced your requests and paid your money, the clerk will give you either one ticket that includes all of your bets or several different tickets. You may request different tickets for each bet, which is invariably a good idea if you've taken somebody else's money to the window to place a bet or two for him or her. Having separate tickets may matter if one of you wins.

When you get your tickets from the clerk, check them immediately to make sure they're exactly what you asked for. You can get a correction as you stand there, but you can't come back later. There are no return privileges in betting on horse races. Once you accept the ticket and walk away, put it in a safe place and enjoy the race.

Some racetracks offer a couple of additional ways to place a bet. You may find a betting machine, or ticket terminal, or whatever the track wants to call it. The machine is like a reverse ATM. You put your money in, punch some buttons according to directions, and get a ticket back.

The machines haven't proven very popular at racetracks or even at off-track betting outlets, and they haven't taken many jobs away from pari-mutuel clerks. That may change someday. The machines provide a quick and efficient way to place a bet.

Kinds of Bets

Some big-money bettors will tell you that the simplest bets aren't worth your time. They don't pay enough, so the argument goes, to be worth the risk that exists every time you put money on a fragile and unstable animal.

Betting a horse to win, place, or show is called *straight wagering,* and there's something to be said for being straight. It's the easiest to do and the most likely to succeed, but it's also usually the least lucrative and—let's face it—the least exciting.

Betting to Win

If you bet a horse to win and only to win, you get a payoff only if the horse actually wins. But, like almost everything else that touches on horse racing, this is not as simple as it appears.

The winner doesn't always have to finish first for you to win your bet. A race is unofficial for a few minutes after the horses cross the finish line. Before it's made official and payoffs become available, the stewards may launch an inquiry into the results, either because of something they've noticed themselves or because of foul claims made by jockeys or drivers. The stewards, after viewing video-tapes and talking to participants, have the option of taking down the winner or any other horse that finishes *in the money.*

From the Horse's Mouth

Finishing **in the money** normally means finishing in the first three positions. But purse money is paid for the first four (and sometimes five) spots, and disqualifications from fourth and fifth are also made regularly.

So don't tear up your tickets in a fit of annoyance when your horse staggers across the finish line. Occasionally, the second- and even third-place horses will find themselves awarded a win because of interference caused by the horse who finished first.

Betting to Place and Show

The advantage of making a straight bet, but not to win, is that you get extra chances for a payoff. If you bet a horse to place (finish second), you get a payoff whether he finishes first or second. If you bet a horse to show (finish third), you collect if he finishes first, second, or third.

The disadvantage of betting to place or show is that the pools, which are separate, must be divided in more ways because there are more people holding tickets eligible for payoffs. That means that the dollar amount of each payoff is usually going to be smaller.

Occasionally, place and show betting can be more lucrative than normal. If a horse of exceptional quality, one heavily favored in the win pool, is inexplicably underbet in the place or show pools, you can anticipate a bigger payoff than the horse deserves. Any horse that's underbet, given his ability and form, is called an *overlay* (an overbet horse is an *underlay*), and it's up to you to find overlays in the win pool. But the tote board can do it for you in the place and show pools.

If the tote board at your track displays regularly updated show and place pools, you may see a horse that has a much smaller percentage of the place and show pools than he deserves. In this case, a place or show bet gives you not only two or three chances to collect, but also the chance of collecting a good chunk of money when you do because you're not going to have to divide it up among so many other ticket holders.

Bad Bet

Other bettors will probably notice the show and place pool overlays, particularly at big racetracks. Don't rely too much on it being a secret. You may see that the percentage of the pool that's bet on the big horse grows as race time approaches. You can hope, though.

The underbet good horse can show up in either the place or show pool, but a win is likely to be much more lucrative if it's in the place pool. Don't reject a dramatically underbet horse in the show pool, but if you're choosing between the two for one bet, choose the bet to place.

Exotics

All exotic wagers have two things in common. They're difficult to figure out, and they can pay extremely well when you do manage to figure them correctly.

Daily Doubles

The oldest and simplest of the exotics is the *daily double*, in which you're asked to pick the winners of two consecutive races, usually the first two of the day. Racetracks happily embraced the concept of the daily double decades ago, as soon as they realized it got people to the racetrack well in advance of the first race.

Many tracks then went on to the *late double*, in which you're asked to pick the winners of the last two races. This kept the fans at the track to the bitter end. Tracks can also offer doubles on any other two races on the card.

The bad news about doubles is that most tracks make sure that at least one of the races involved in each double features large fields of horses that are extremely hard to figure. Maiden claiming races designed for the worst horses in the barns are a particular favorite for the second race in a double.

Because of the unlikelihood that both races in a double will be easy to figure, most serious bettors in doubles work some kind of a *wheel* into their wager. A daily double wheel might consist of the horse you're confident of in the second race, combined with separate bets on every horse in the first race. That's a lot of bets, possibly costing more than you can recoup even if your horse in the second race does win.

From the Horse's Mouth

In a **wheel,** a bettor picks one sure horse and then places bets on every other possible combination for the other horse. You're sure of horse #6? You wheel #6 with the rest of the field. You place separate bets for each possible combination.

Exactas

These bets, called *perfectas* at some tracks, are second in popularity only to daily doubles. Most racetracks take exacta wagering on almost every race.

To win an exacta, you have to pick the first and second finishers in one race in exact order. The bet isn't especially lucrative if the top two choices finish first and second, usually only about double what you'd collect if you had a win ticket on the winner and a place ticket on the second-place horse. Of course, your single exacta bet would cost you half as much as your two separate tickets. *Boxing* is a favored betting tactic in exactas when you're sure of horses but not sure of precisely where they'll finish.

From the Horse's Mouth

You **box** a bet when you cover every combination of two or more horses with separate bets. An exacta box using the #1 and #2 horses consists of two separate bets: the #1 winning and the #2 finishing second in one bet, and the #2 winning and #1 finishing second in the other.

Quinellas

A *quinella* (sometimes spelled *quiniella*) wager will take care of boxing for you, and it will only cost you the price of a single bet. This wager requires you to pick two horses to finish first and second in any order. It's about twice as easy to win as an exacta and tends to pay about half as much.

The quinella isn't as widely offered as the exacta, probably because it doesn't have the same potential for big money payoffs. Tracks, too, would probably prefer that people box exactas rather than bet quinellas because the track makes more money that way.

You box three horses in a quinella. In other words, you bet 1 and 2, 1 and 3, and 2 and 3. In a $2 quinella, that's $6 in bets. If any of the three finish first and second, you'll win your quinella bet, and it will certainly pay more than $6.

Trifectas

In this bet, also called a triple, you're required to pick the first three finishers in exact order. The payoffs can be extremely high if a long shot finishes anywhere in the top three. Unfortunately, the trifecta is also extremely difficult to win. What's difficult is figuring in the effect of the random events that plague every horse race. Bettors solve the problem by boxing. There's probably more of it in this kind of wager than any other. Using a $2 trifecta bet as an example, here's what boxing does and costs.

Trifecta box using horses 1, 2, and 3, covering every order in which they can finish

1-2-3	$2.00
1-3-2	$2.00
2-1-3	$2.00
2-3-1	$2.00
3-1-2	$2.00
3-2-1	$2.00
	$12.00 for 6 separate bets

If you're a little less sure and want to add a fourth horse to the mix, that will work out to 24 separate bets totaling $48.00.

The problem with boxing trifectas is clear: It's expensive. If you don't want to make six separate bets, use this compromise method of playing a trifecta:

➤ Pick your winner and put him on top of your trifecta ticket.

➤ Pick two more horses and box them in second and third place, so you'll have a 1-2-3 trifecta and a 1-3-2 trifecta. That's $4 worth of tickets. If you have no idea who's going to win, put the $4 into a hot dog and fries while the race is being run.

Some tracks offer what they call *superfectas,* in which you're supposed to pick the first four horses in order. Everything that's true of trifectas is super-true of superfectas, including the amount of money necessary to box horses. Most people will find that their time is better spent picking winners than working out possible superfecta bets.

Pick-Six (or –Three, or –Four)

These bets call for picking winners in six (or three or four) straight races. Not every track offers them. Needless to say, they're difficult to win, but serious bettors often put a couple of dollars on them whenever they're offered. They're appealing for several reasons:

➤ The payoff tends to be the biggest available at the racetrack, especially if a long shot or two figures into the list of winners.

➤ Even when nobody wins, a decent consolation prize goes to the near-winners, at least for the pick-sixes.

➤ When nobody wins the big prize, the money in the pool carries over to the next day, creating huge pools that sometimes last for weeks.

➤ Because most people pick potential winners before they figure any other kind of betting, they feel they might as well place a single bet on all their choices. It's a cheap thrill.

On the other side of the argument, some bettors believe that pick-whatevers are poor bets because of the following:

➤ Even if random and unexpected happenings don't occur in one or even two races, you can be sure they will in the next one.

➤ Whether they mean to or not, racing secretaries seem to place at least one race right into the middle of the schedule, in which, on paper, not a single horse is good enough to win. (They probably mean to.)

➤ Some races, whether they feature good horses or bad, should never be bet on because the patterns aren't clear.

Chapter 12

Get with the Program (and the Past Performances)

In This Chapter

➤ What's in the program

➤ Why you need the past performances

➤ What's in each

Think of them as the map to Captain Kidd's treasure, plus the key to help you interpret that map. They're better known as the *program* and the *past performances*. You used to need both to succeed at the racetrack or even to understand what was going on. Today, the two documents tend to overlap, and it's sometimes possible to get by with one or the other. Let's start with the most important and fundamental one.

The Program

Every racetrack publishes its own program, a different one for each day of racing. In every program, no matter how cheap the track and small its publication, you'll find basic data, some of which you can happily overlook. Other information is vital if you expect to bet successfully.

Most racetrack programs only cost a dollar or two, and it's well worth the investment even though most of the same data will also be in any past performance publication that you purchase. The following information is included in every program:

➤ The names of track officers, stewards, and other people whose identities are more important to those who work at the track than those who bet on the horses. Pay attention to these names only if you're looking for someone to whom to address a complaint about the quality of the food.

➤ Conditions for each race on the card. These are listed at the top of the page devoted to the race and include purse, distance, and claiming price, as well as the age, sex, and any race record limitations of the horses permitted to be entered. In Thoroughbred and Quarter Horse racing, the information also includes the base weight to be carried, plus provisions for weight allowances. If the race is on the turf, that information is included here, too.

➤ The list of entered horses, plus the numbers they're going to wear on their saddlecloths. In most cases, the horses' numbers coincide with their places in the starting gate, with the lowest numbers nearest the rail. You may find an additional number with the letters *PP* next to the horse's name. The plain number is the horse's saddlecloth number; the *PP* number is his post position.

➤ A description of the horse, including his age, sex, and color.

➤ The horse's sire and dam.

➤ A description of the jacket colors worn by the jockey or driver.

➤ The weight to be carried by the individual horse (in Thoroughbred and Quarter Horse racing).

➤ The name of the jockey or driver.

➤ The name of the trainer.

➤ The name of the owner.

➤ *Morning line* odds.

➤ The kind of wagering permitted on the race.

From the Horse's Mouth

The **morning line** is the predicted odds breakdown of the race. The oddsmaker isn't predicting the finish; he's guessing what the real bettors are going to do.

Slightly more complete basic programs give you the following (either on or apart from the pages devoted to the race entries):

➤ A selection of track records so you can judge as the race day progresses just how fast the horses are going.

➤ A description of the wagering process.

➤ A diagram of the racetrack, showing you the location of the starting gate for each race distance.

➤ Current jockey and trainer standings, including starts and placements.

➤ Statistics on winning percentages of each post position.

➤ Early entries for the following day.

Extremely complete programs add the following information:

➤ Past performance charts for each horse entered in each race.

➤ Choices of one or more handicappers (other than the morning line oddsmaker).

➤ Tips on how to win at the races.

➤ Interesting statistics, such as the most successful jockeys on the turf, the best trainers in claiming races, and so forth.

Past Performances

For decades, harness racing's policy has been for the racetracks to provide programs with almost all the information a bettor needs; flat tracks have expected bettors to buy past performance publications. Almost all harness programs include a reasonable selection of past performances, as well as each horse's lifetime statistics for victories, earnings, and speed records. Most programs also include tables for track variants, so you can adequately compare times earned at different tracks.

The tradition probably developed because there's no harness equivalent of the *Daily Racing Form,* at least in terms of its hundred-year history and database. There is *Sports Eye,* a past performance publication whose information is every bit as good as the *Form's,* but its presence has never been quite as pervasive in the harness sport as the

Form has been in Thoroughbred racing, and harness tracks have always felt it necessary to provide at least modest past performance data themselves.

A few years ago, some Thoroughbred tracks decided to get into the past performance business. Some wanted to break the stranglehold of the *Daily Racing Form* on racing data; others simply realized that fans like a program that tells them more than the basics. Many flat tracks are now providing past performances in their programs.

Most Thoroughbred racetracks and simulcast betting outlets get their past performance data from Equibase, a company that was formed by the Jockey Club and the Thoroughbred Racing Association, an organization of racetracks. The Equibase data and past performance charts have much in common with those of the *Daily Racing Form*, although there are slight differences.

Deciphering the PPs

If you hope to win at the races, not just enjoy them, you have to learn to read and understand past performance charts, also known as the *PPs*. It doesn't matter whether you get them from the track program or from one of the specialty publications.

All of the basic program information, except possibly for the colors of horses and jackets, can play some part in your betting decisions. We've talked in previous chapters about the importance of the various characteristics of horses, humans, and racetracks. Some attributes matter a great deal, some very little, but none matter as much as the information you'll find in the past performance charts.

Remember about Captain Kidd and how the PPs are the map to the buried treasure? That's not entirely accurate. The PPs are more like the buried treasure itself. Hidden in the tiny lines of type (bring your reading glasses) are the secrets of a horse's soundness, speed, and stamina. They tell you if he's in the kind of race he can reasonably expect to win or if he's in over his head. They give you hints (although not firm proof) about whether he's in condition to live up to his potential.

Almost anything you might want to know about a race-horse is right there, but you have to do a little digging to find some of it. No matter which source of past perfor-mances you use, you'll find most of the same information, although the publishers offer exclusive items that they hope will convince you that you must buy their product if you want to win.

The charts are divided by race, with one set of past perfor-mances for each race. The set includes information about every horse entered in the race. In past performance publi-cations such as the *Daily Racing Form* and *Sports Eye,* note that the top of the set of charts for each race includes the same basic information that you'll see in the program. You'll see the conditions of the race, the qualifications for entry, the purse, the type of wagers to be accepted, the length, and—if it's a Thoroughbred race—the racing surface. For harness horses, you'll see whether the race is a trot or a pace.

In these details, the PP is like the program. But past performance charts, whether they're part of an elaborate track-produced program or a specialized publication, go further.

By the way, the *Daily Racing Form* has recently undergone a change in ownership. There may be changes in its past performance formatting and statistics, but most of the traditional information should remain.

Jockey, Driver, and Trainer Statistics

What statistics you see depends on the sport and the publication. In Thoroughbred and Quarter Horse racing, you find the name of the jockey plus a number indicating any apprentice allowance that he claims. The *Daily Racing Form* prints a summary of his starts and finishes, plus a figure that indicates winning percentage. For most races, you'll see two sets of figures. The first is for the current race meet, and the second is a less complete summary for the year to date. The jockey statistics look like this:

SHAKESPEARE, W (49 8 6 6 .16) 1999:
(1149 164 .14)

This line means that Willie Shakespeare has ridden in 49 races in the current meet at Avon Downs, of which he's won 8, finished second in 6, and finished third in another 6. He's won 16 percent of his races. In 1999, Willie has started 1,149 races, of which he's won 164 for 14 percent. It's been a pretty average year for Willie.

The *Form* also prints extensive jockey charts elsewhere in the publication, telling you things such as a jockey's performance in sprints, in routes, with favorites, on the turf, and more.

Racetracks that use Equibase past performances vary in how much jockey information they print in the program, whether on the PP page or elsewhere. The stats they do offer will probably appear in a format similar to the *Form*'s.

In harness racing, driver statistics are always a vital part of past performance charts. Complete driver statistics look like this:

Driver GEOFF CHAUCER 150 (red/blk)
(771-135-111-92-.295)

Geoff, who's having an excellent year, weighs 150 pounds and will be wearing red and black. He's started 771 races, with 135 wins, 111 seconds, and 92 thirds. The last figure is not winning percentage as in flat racing; it's the

Universal Driver Rating (UDR). See Chapter 7 for an explanation of UDR. Some tracks and publications also include Geoff's birth date, making it impossible for him to lie about much.

In both flat and harness racing, some past performance charts also include the statistics enjoyed by the horse's trainer, although not his weight and age.

The Horse

All past performance charts also include summaries of the horse's racing careers, printing breakdowns of entries, placements, and earnings for some combination of the current year, the past year, and the horse's entire racing career. In flat racing, it will look something like this:

> 1999 9 2 2 1 $101,502

This horse has started nine times, won two, finished second twice, third once, and earned $101,502 in 1999. His next line shows you that he's not improving:

> 1998 6 4 3 1 $295,713

Then comes his lifetime record:

> Life: 18 8 7 3 $492,105

Most past performance charts add similar breakdowns for the horse's performances on turf courses and on wet tracks. The *Daily Racing Form* adds the horse's record over the current track and at the distance of today's race.

Bad Bet

Take good wet track stats with a grain of salt. There are sloppy wet tracks, hard and fast wet tracks, and everything in between. Look down the charts to try to see what kind of wet track the horse has excelled on before concluding that he'll be good in today's mud.

In harness racing, charts include the starts and placing percentages, and they add a statistic that's vital in determining a horse's quality: his best mile time for the year. Some programs include his best mile time from the previous year, his best lifetime mile time, or both. These times appear on the same line as the win-loss statistics, either to the right or left. A harness horse's record might appear like this:

1999: 14 3 2 4 $37,502 1:54 M 1

This horse, that's won 3 of 14 starts in 1999, went a mile in 1 minute 54 seconds at the Meadowlands Racetrack, a one-mile oval. You'll find a chart identifying the racetrack symbols elsewhere in the program or the past performance publication. The size of the track matters because harness horses race faster over the larger tracks. You'd be more impressed if you saw a $5/8$ for a $5/8$-mile track or no symbol at all, which means the track was $1/2$ mile around.

Next, and most important, are the lines describing each horse's previous races. The various publications each use slightly different formats, but learning to read one ensures that you can read the others. Here's the first third of a typical line, reading left to right:

> 19Sep98 SA 8 6F ft :22 :44 :56 1:09 3U Clm12000

Translation: The horse last raced on September 19, 1998, in the eighth race of that day at Santa Anita. The race, 6 furlongs in length, took place on a fast track.

Track Condition Symbols

Symbol	Meaning
Main Track	
ft (fast)	Hard and dry
gd (good)	A little soft and maybe damp
sly (sloppy)	Wet, but probably still hard underneath
my (muddy)	Wet and soft
Turf Course	
fm (firm)	Not too dry and not too wet
gd (good)	A little soft and damp
yl (yielding)	A little softer and damper

In past performance lines for European races, you're likely to see hd (hard) and sf (soft).

Next come the running times of the horse leading the race (not necessarily the horse you're examining) at the points of call. In this race, you're looking at the leader's running time at the $1/4$ mile, the $1/2$ mile, the stretch (about 5 furlongs), and the finish. Next, you discover that the race was for three-year-olds and up (you may see an arrow pointing upward rather than a U), and that the race was a claiming event with a price tag of $25,000 for entries.

The *Daily Racing Form* and the Equibase programs differ in the next notation. In the *Form*, you'll see a double-digit number in boldface; it's the *Beyer Speed Index*, a figure worked out according to a formula developed by *Washington Post* columnist and horseplayer extraordinaire Andrew Beyer. The figure is designed to quantify the quality of speed shown by the horse in the race, taking into account not only the time of the race, the distance he finished behind, but track biases and conditions for the day.

Following the Speed Index comes the horse's positions at the calls of the race. The middle third of the line will look like this:

$$5\ 2\ 3^{hd}\ 4^{1/2}\ 5^{1}5^{2}\ \text{Shakespeare.W L118 3.60}$$

The horse, who broke out of post position 5, jumped out of the starting gate in second place, dropped back to third after the first quarter, moved up to fourth at the ½ mile, and was fifth in mid-stretch, where he remained at the finish. The superscript shows his distance in *lengths* behind the horse in front of him.

From the Horse's Mouth

A **length** is a horse's body length, minus his neck and head.

Willie Shakespeare rode our horse in the race. The animal was given Lasix (see Chapter 3) prior to the race, and he was assigned 118 pounds. Some past performance charts place the medication symbol after rather than before the weight assignment. Our horse started the race at odds of 3.60 to 1.

The final third of the line might look like this:

> (82-14) or (93) Hamlet[1] [1/2], Macbeth[2], King Lear[1] bid, hung stretch 12

First comes one of two speed figures. The *Form,* in addition to the Beyer figure, offers a less precise assessment of the speed of the race. The first half of the double figure (82 in this case) represents the horse's time in relation to the track record (that would be 100), and the second half represents the track variant for the day. The total of the two is the figure you'll use. In this case, the horse gets a 96.

The Equibase program past performances include the second figure, a Speed Index similar in intent to the Beyer Index. Again, highest is best. This horse ran a pretty quick race last time out in spite of his fifth-place finish and gets a 93 by the Beyer method.

The three names that follow are the first three horses in order of finish, followed by the lengths they finished in front of the next horse. The word *bid* indicates that our horse made a run at the leaders but was unable to make up ground in the stretch and *hung.* Finally, we discover that there were 12 horses in the race, making our horse's fifth-place finish a little more impressive.

From the Horse's Mouth

Past performance comments are usually self-evident. Among the comments that might mean the performance was better than it looked: **checked** (had to slow down to avoid traffic), **impeded** (his progress was affected by another horse), **taken up** (his jockey came close to stopping him to avoid a collision), and **wide** (he lost ground and ran farther than the rest of the field).

At the bottom of each horse's array of previous races you'll find information about his most recent public workouts. See Chapter 2 for a discussion of workouts and what they mean in terms of speed and readiness.

In Quarter Horse racing, the past performance line is similar, except there are fewer interim times and positions because most of the races are much shorter. In the average sub–quarter-mile race, the first number indicates how the horse broke out of the gate. It's the number (other than finishing position) that means the most. Some Quarter Horse past performances also include information on any head or tail wind that might have affected the final time.

In steeplechasing, you also see fewer calls and may see little indication of interim time and distances. In jump racing, horses tend to string themselves out, making the assessment of leads difficult.

In harness racing, the data is supplied to tracks by the United States Trotting Association. You'll find past performance lines similar to what you find in Thoroughbred charts, with a few exceptions:

➤ Harness PPs include the final time for the horse in question, no matter where he finished. You don't have to extrapolate from the winning time and the lengths behind. It's printed right there for you to use.

➤ Both purse and claiming price of previous races are included, giving you a better assessment of the quality of the race.

➤ There's no equivalent of the jockey's weight.

➤ Because each track produces its own program, you'll find that some charts include comments on the race, and some don't.

From the Horse's Mouth

These are some of the harness comments you may see: **cvr** (the horse raced behind another horse, providing him cover and less wind resistance) and **ruff** (rough gaited). The comments that indicate a better effort than the finish would suggest are **Equip** (equipment problem), **unc** (uncovered), **wd** (wide).

The harness line also includes symbols to tell you any trouble the horse may have had during the course of the race. These symbols are important to note because you can assume a horse who had a troubled race would have raced faster with a cleaner race. What you're looking for is x's and o's.

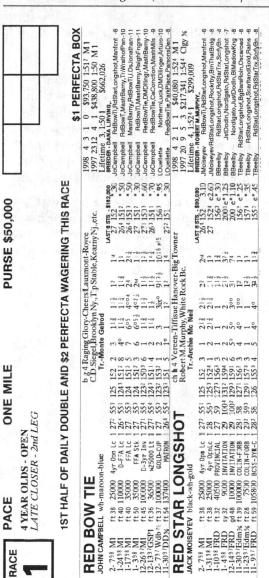

Here's a typical past performance page as compiled by the United States Trotting Association.

This section of the line shows the horse's position at various points of the race:

$$6\ 6^0\ 7^{005}\ 6^x\ 12\ 12^{9\ 1/2}$$

This unfortunate horse should have stayed in the barn. He was forced wide shortly after the start, and then was pushed two horses wide at the $1/4$-mile mark. At $1/2$ mile, while running 6th, he broke stride. His driver was forced to drop him back to 12th, where he stayed to the finish. He crossed the finish line 9 $1/2$ lengths behind the winner.

But before you assume too much about his potential, take a look further back in his past performances. Some horses are better at finding bad racing luck than they are at finding the winner's circle. Make sure he's not a horse who's always in trouble.

Chapter 13

Super Systems and Marvelous Methods

Here's a likely scenario: You've studied the horses' appearance, their behavior, their breeding, and their past performances. You've looked at the skills of their trainers and their riders or drivers. You've analyzed the conditions of the race and the racetrack, and you've discovered one of two things:

➤ Every horse in the race appears to have a chance to win.

➤ No horse in the race appears to have a chance to win.

Two additional things then happen:

➤ The racing secretary does private handstands, having written a highly competitive race.

➤ Bettors do public handwringing, being unable to separate the contenders and place their bets with confidence.

The dilemma is solved by a System, sometimes printed or spoken with a capital *S* (feel free to call it a Method, with a capital *M*). A System isn't magic, and it provides no guarantees, but it does help you separate horses without devoting every waking hour to your decision-making process.

Mostly Mindless Methods

You have two ready-made systems to call upon for your betting choices. In each of them, you can take the choice and make no further decisions yourself. You will get a respectable number of winners this way, but you'll probably lose money in the long run (and even in the not-so-long run). Or you can modify these systems, using some of the techniques mentioned later in this chapter.

Bet the Favorite

The betting public is pretty good at predicting winners. Unfortunately, the betting favorites also have the shortest odds, so the ones who win for you probably won't pay enough to make up for the ones who lose for you.

Your Favorites System might be this:

➤ Bet favorites, but only when they're tops in one of the other categories upon which more specialized systems are based.

➤ Bet favorites, but only when their odds are higher than 3-2, 2-1, or whichever you choose.

Bet the Consensus

The *consensus* is the best bet in the race, figured by averaging the choices of a group of handicappers working for a newspaper or past performance publication. The consensus is usually the favorite, and his payoffs probably won't be high enough to make up for his losses. But he differs from the favorite in that he's the pick of at least three racing specialists, people who aren't likely to be overly influenced by the name of the jockey, trainer, or anything other than potential performance.

Your Consensus System might be this:

➤ Bet the consensus, but only when he's second or third choice in one of the other systems.

➤ Bet the consensus, but sit out the race when he's not the top choice in at least one of the other systems.

The Sensible Systems

Serious bettors use hundreds of systems, some more successfully than others, but almost all systems fit into just a few general categories. You will also find systems that take the Chinese dinner approach, selecting a point from one system, a couple of points from another, and a tiebreaker from a third. Will decisions never end?

Speed

Because the race goes to the horse that gets to the finish line first, systems that use speed as the primary factor lead the list of categories. Speed's importance is recognized in each of the racing sports. In Quarter Horse racing, speed is almost everything. A horse *is* his speed. If he's fast, he wins. If he's slow, he loses.

In Standardbred racing, speed is almost everything. Throughout his life, he'll be identified by his best-ever time for a mile. Tar Heel wasn't just Tar Heel. He was Tar Heel (1:57 ^{2}/$_5$).

In Thoroughbred racing, speed is a little more ambiguous. There are so many variables in distance, track design, weight carried, and so on that a lot of very intelligent people spend considerable time developing figures that are supposed to quantify race times. These figures have become so well-respected that past performance publications offer dueling numbers in order to sell copies.

A well-designed method of determining figures manages to factor out weather, track bias, and things that make both the final and fractional times of races misleading. The figures make sure that you don't look at a race in a past performance line, see a ploddingly slow final time, and assume that the horse can't outrun a Budweiser Clydesdale.

Refer to Chapter 12 for information on where you can find the most useful (and free for the price of a past performance publication) figures. Use them in a system like this one, the simplest of all for figures users:

From the Horse's Mouth

Speed figures are often called **figs**, and people who use them to bet are called **fig players.**

➤ Bet the horse with the highest printed speed figures, either total or average, over his past three races (use three races to eliminate the chance of an aberration that can occur with even the most careful figures).

But speed figures, no matter how carefully computed, lose their effectiveness in certain situations, making them a little less simple than they appear. The problems occur when:

➤ The current race is substantially different in length from previous ones. Although figures are worked out so that distance isn't supposed to matter, you simply can't assume that a horse will run well or poorly when he tries a new distance.

➤ Either the current race or the previous ones take place on an unusually wet or dry track. Yes, the figures take into account how slow or fast the track is on the day of the race, but there's no way you can quantify a horse's individual reaction to the feel of the track surface under his hoofs. He may hate to slip; he may enjoy splashing; he may hurt on a hard, dry track.

➤ Either the current race or the ones that provided the figures are $1^1/8$ mile or longer. Speed figures lose their importance as distances increase because pure speed becomes less significant.

If you choose not to put your faith in figures, you can still use speed to develop betting systems. This system for the most common sprint distances is based on the fact that a horse with enough natural speed to get to or near the lead early has a good chance of holding on for a win, but a slower horse that has to come from behind more often fails.

➤ Examine each horse's last three races on fast or good tracks.

➤ Write down the horse's position at the first two calls in each of the races. Add the numbers (if he was second and third in one race, first and fourth in another, and sixth and fourth in the third, his total is 20).

➤ If two or more horses have the same numbers, adjust by subtracting 3 points for each race the horse won, 2 points for second place, and 1 for third.

➤ The lowest point total gets your money.

Another method uses the kind of speed that enables a horse to gain ground in the stretch. But don't neglect the value of early speed. Look for a horse who, in his last race:

➤ Was leading or was within 3 lengths of the lead at the first and second calls, and...

➤ Who gained at least 1 length between the final call at the middle of the stretch and the finish line, and...

➤ Who finished either in the money or within 6 lengths of the winner.

If there's more than one horse who qualifies:

➤ Look at the next-to-last races to try to find a horse who's gained ground more than once.

➤ If there's still a tie, choose the higher placed finish if the class of the race is similar.

In each of these nonfigure speed systems, it is worth your while to check your choice with the figure choice. If you and the numbers agree, the horse is a particularly appealing bet.

In harness racing, almost everybody who employs a sensible system of picking winners uses speed as the primary differentiator. Almost all races are one mile, making time comparisons far easier than they are in Thoroughbred racing. Even the differences in track speed are quantified in almost every program and all past performance publications. You'll find the chart displayed prominently, along with a key to figure a par speed for a race you're studying. You may find, for example, that if your horse raced a 2:01 mile at Freehold Raceway and his main competition raced 2:02 at Yonkers, you need to subtract $^2/_5$ second from your horse's time to get a fair comparison.

Here's the simplest harness speed system of all:

1. Write down each horse's final times in his last three races.

2. Adjust them according to the track variants published in your past performance charts.

3. Average the times, and the horse with the fastest mile gets your money.

This super simple system works best in the following situations:

➤ When the previous races were on one-mile race-tracks (less chance of interference on the big tracks means the final times represent race speed more accurately).

➤ When the horse who comes out first in the figures won his previous race or races going most of the way in front, suggesting that his time wasn't a result of being *sucked along* by a faster horse in front of him. It also suggests that he might have gone even faster if he had been pressed.

From the Horse's Mouth

A harness horse that races directly behind another is **sucked along** to a faster speed than he'd earn by his efforts because he enjoys less wind resistance. A horse that's **parked** is forced to race wide.

➤ When there isn't evidence of rough races or other trouble, such as the *parked* symbol (⁰) or other signs of interference.

You'll find that times in most previous races need to be adjusted, at least a little. Two examples:

➤ If the horse was parked, he covered extra ground, and you must take a fraction off his time to get an accurate picture of how fast he went. Here's a rough formula: A horse who has one ⁰ was forced to travel a whole extra horse and sulky wider than the others. If you see that at the 1/2-mile mark, take ²/₅ of a second off his final time. Take another ²/₅ of a second off for additional ⁰ symbols.

➤ Give the horse a little extra credit for a poor post position when the race took place on a ¹/₂-mile or ⁵/₈-mile track. Give no additional time off for PPs 1 through 4, take off ³/₅ of a second for 5 through 7, and take off a full second for any PP above 7.

Form and Condition Systems

A horse has to be in good physical and mental condition to use his speed effectively. It doesn't matter how much talent he has or how good he used to be. He has to be good enough *now*.

Current condition matters so much that some Thoroughbred bettors use a system that says:

> Bet the horse with the fastest recent workout, particularly if it's a bullet (the fastest of the day).

This system assures you that you put your money on a horse who's both fast and ready. Of course, this system presumes that the workout was accurately timed and that it was at a racing distance, not the more common short workout distance.

Other bettors believe that form is different from condition, and they ask more of their systems. They want not just physical readiness, but also real-life proof that their bet is on a horse who's ready to race.

Some systems pay so much attention to the real world that the first step is this one unbreakable rule:

> Bet on no horse that hasn't started in the last 30 days.

You miss a few very good, pampered horses by following this rule, but you probably save a lot of money that you might have put on ones not at their peak.

Inside Track

Although you usually shouldn't bet a horse in his first race after a long layoff, he's often ready for the performance of his life in his second start after a break.

Some bettors believe in recent racing so much that their system for picking winners goes on to say simply:

Bet the horse with the best recent performance.

Here's a slightly more elaborate, step-by-step procedure for a system based on current form and condition:

1. Count the days since the last start for each horse.

2. Add that to the number of the horse's finish in the race.

3. The lowest total gets your bet. Example: A third-place finish 7 days ago equals 10 points. A second-place finish 14 days ago equals 16 points. The 10-pointer wins.

This system, like all very simple systems, works best when there's little difference between the current race and previous ones in terms of class, track, weather, and so forth.

Here's another system whose simplicity is both virtue and vice. It's designed to pick a horse whose form is improving:

1. Write down each horse's finish in his last three races.

2. Pick out the horse whose last finish was an improvement on his next-to-last.

3. If there's a tie, pick the horse whose finish in his third race back was an improvement over his next-to-last.

Some very expensive tip sheets offer an examination of each horse's racing career in terms of the circumstances surrounding his best performances. Their goal is to spotlight those horses that reach for a big bounce in performance. The race analysts who produce the *sheets* look at every race in a horse's career, not just the 6 to 10 included in past performance charts.

From the Horse's Mouth

If you hear somebody claim that the **sheets** say a horse is ready, they're referring to the high-priced analysis publications, not the cheap tip sheets that give you four selections in a six-horse field.

These tip sheets identify career-long patterns: Does a horse tail off in performance after five races? Does he bounce after a 60-day layoff and then two mediocre prep races? People who can afford a thousand dollars or more a year to subscribe swear by them, but you have to wonder why their publishers aren't just keeping the information for themselves.

Class

Some systems rely most heavily on looking at the class of the horses' previous races, the class of the current race, and figuring out what the differences between the two might mean to the outcome of the race. The simplest class betting system is this:

> Pick the horses dropping down in class from their last races.

The rationale here is that a horse that's used to running against better horses will be overjoyed at the softer competition and will dominate them. The great weakness in this system is that horses usually drop in class (purses and claiming price drop along with class) only when they can't win at the next higher level. If you bet on a drop-down, you're betting on a horse in the habit of losing.

To be fair, most horses do have an easier time the first time they face lower-class horses, but it's difficult to figure out if the horse is dropping because he can't quite handle the next level up or because he has such a physical or behavioral problem that he's not going to win at any level. Some people who glorify class choose another approach. Their system says that money talks:

> Pick the horse who has the highest average earnings per start over his lifetime. Divide the total lifetime earnings (printed in all past performance charts) by the number of starts. Money is a pretty good indicator of class because the highest purses go to the highest class races.

If several of the horses earned the bulk of their money more than one year ago, modify the system like this:

> Pick the horse who has the highest average earnings per start over his last six starts. This system is a little harder because it probably requires that you do some adding yourself, but it gives you a better idea of current class than the lifetime figure.

Finally, here's a method that helps you pick a horse who's ready. It's based on the class of the horse's recent company, but it's the opposite of the first class-based betting system.

> Pick a horse that's moving up in class.

What? You pick a horse that's about to face more difficult competition? Yes, and here's why. A horse who's moving into tougher competition is doing it because his connections believe he's in good form, good condition, and he's too good to risk at a lower claiming price. That's certainly a vote of confidence from the people who know him best.

To make sure he's not moving up because of trainer and owner delusions, look for this in the horse moving into better company:

➤ A win or close finish in his last start.

➤ No big increase in assigned weight, especially if the race is one mile or more. It's too much to ask a horse to beat faster horses carrying a heavier weight at the same time.

➤ As a tiebreaker: a start in a previous race, even a while ago, at the new class level.

Trip

Trip handicappers are bettors looking for trouble. Their systems are based on finding horses whose past performances were better than they look because of problems they encountered during the races.

This approach can certainly help you find horses whose odds are longer than they should be, given the horse's form and talent. It can also help you find unexpected winners because the horse may have been dropped down to softer competition in an effort to change his luck.

Trip handicapping doesn't offer a system, but it does give you guidelines to consider when looking for a likely bet. Here's the procedure:

➤ Examine each horse's past two or three races to see what kind of racing experiences he had.

➤ Look first for trouble. It's easier in harness than in Thoroughbred racing because the symbols are included at each point on the race line. Refer to Chapter 12 for details on this.

➤ Look for indications that the horse raced well in spite of the trouble. You may see evidence that a horse ran well early, dropped back while losing ground, and then moved up again. He probably had racing trouble from which he recovered.

➤ After examining the charts, give a horse coming off a troubled race credit for being at least a little better than his finish or speed figures indicated.

➤ If he finished well, give him a lot of credit.

➤ If he appeared to have an untroubled race, racing on or near the lead the whole way, and still couldn't hold on, take away credit.

The Combo System

If you're serious about winning at the races, systems based exclusively on one category are a little too simple. A fast horse has the best chance, but a determined one, a sound one, or even a lucky one can often beat him. Class is nice, but many a fine stakes horse ends his career struggling against cheap claimers because of injury or age. You have to pay attention to trips, but a bad trip in a previous race doesn't turn a slow horse fast. All it will help you do is get longer odds in a bet on him.

If you had the time, you might figure each race with simple systems from each category and then pick the horse that came out on top in the most systems. Or you might try this quick system to pick winners, taking factors from most of the categories. Analyze each horse like this:

➤ Quantify form by writing down the horse's finish in his last three races, and then add those three numbers. If he's finished second, fourth, and first, his number is 7.

➤ Quantify condition by writing down the number of days the horse has been away from the races. A horse who last started a week ago gets a 7. This rule is a little unfair to high-quality horses who are asked for fewer races, but it's a useful standard in the vast majority of races.

➤ Quantify speed by writing down the number of lengths the horse finished behind the winner. (A winner gets a 0.)

➤ Quantify class by adding the odds to one the horse enjoyed in his last three races (you may have to break down some of the odds to a factor of one). 4-1, 3-2, and 2-1 equals 7 $\frac{1}{2}$.

➤ Add all the figures for each horse. The horse with the lowest total gets your money.

Notice that there are no speed figures, no attempt to assign numbers to different classes of races, and no race times. This system's attraction is its ease and quickness. It also shows that you can develop any system you like, using any combination of points from the categories. Try it. You may discover the best and most effective one of all.

Chapter 14

Money Matters

In This Chapter

➤ Progression money management

➤ Percentage wagering

➤ Parlays

➤ Hedging your bets

➤ Dutching

Let's pause for a minute to admire the people who can go to the racetrack, enjoy the races, bet on a few of them (because it really is more fun that way), and go home, writing off their net losses as the price of enjoyment. Let's admire them, but let's not spend too much time trying to emulate them. Unless you're happy to lose money, you can't be quite so lackadaisical about it. It's hard to pick winners, and it's even harder to make money when you bet on them.

How to Lose Even When You Win

The shadow known as takeout darkens every betting transaction you make, and to keep the gloomy metaphor going, you have to get out from under its murky depths if you hope to break even, much less win. The evil twins of takeout and breakage see to it that 15 to 20 percent of the betting pool is spirited away before the money is distributed to the winning bettors.

The result is that you have to make sure that your winning bets give you at least 15 to 20 percent profit on those bets, plus enough additional profit to make up for all the bets that you lose altogether. You *will* lose races; even the world's best handicapper isn't going to pick more than about 35 percent winners and 80 percent in-the-money finishers.

Making enough profit on your wins is a tall order because most of those 35 percent winners (more like 30 for normal people) are going to be favorites with modest payoffs. To make a profit of any kind, you need to pick more than a good share of winners. You need to manage the money you bring to the racetrack with caution, common sense, and a little bit of courage.

Your goal is this: You must win more when you win, and you must lose less when you lose. And you must make sure that you have enough money left to enjoy all the races you hope to. There are methods and systems to help you do this. First, though, some basic and essential rules.

The Golden Rules of Racetrack Betting

These rules aren't much fun because they're designed to minimize your losses rather than maximize your wins. Follow them anyway, or else you won't have the money to try to win with.

Rule #1: Don't Bet Every Race

Some races are so difficult to handicap that it's not worth your time to handicap them and not worth your money to bet on them. If you simply can't enjoy your day at the races if you don't have a little something on each race, rank the races according to the confidence you have in your selections: those you think you've figured, those you hope you've figured, and those you have no idea about. Bet the most you can afford, be it $10, $20, or whatever, on the races in the first group. Halve that for the races in the second group, and put the minimum the track allows on races in the third group.

From the Horse's Mouth

A **spot play** is a bet on a race that fits certain characteristics. A sensible bettor puts his money into spot plays, not an entire race card.

Rule #2: Don't Go Into Debt to Bet

If you take your cash advance credit card to the track, you're almost guaranteed to lose, even if you win some bets. Not only does the interest on the credit card, added to the takeout, make it almost impossible for you to make a profit, but you'll also keep doing it until you lose big. If you don't have it, don't bet it.

Rule #3: Quit While You're Ahead

This is what you're supposed to do whenever you bet, whatever you bet on. It's also the hardest rule to follow because it's human nature to want to repeat successes. It's also the nature of racing to make you believe (because it's true) that your skill and not just luck contributed to your win. So it's even harder to walk away from the window.

Do it anyway; you can use this method to help you. Decide before the first race exactly how much money you can realistically hope to win, given your bankroll and the looks of the races. Count your money after each race, and the moment you reach your goal, stop betting. Tell yourself that the satisfaction of reaching the goal is yet another win. (This works, if you're loud enough with yourself.)

Now, on to the systems for money management.

Being Progressive

Most of the systems you'll hear about involve what's known as *progressions*. Being progressive sounds very sensible, but the system sounds a lot less reasonable when you realize that it requires you to bet more after you've lost a race and less after you've won.

Actually, there is reason behind the concept. Progressive betting is supposed to allow you to recoup your losses after a series of losing bets, which—by all statistics—are likely to be more frequent than winning ones. The following table shows how progressive betting is supposed to work, using a flat $2 win bet as an example. You add $2 to your bet after every losing race, dropping back to your original $2 after you win.

Progressive Betting

Race 1	Bet $2 to win	Lose
Race 2	Bet $4 to win	Lose
Race 3	Bet $6 to win	Lose
Race 4	Bet $8 to win	Win
Race 5	Bet $2 to win	?

The theory is this: Although you lose more races than you win when you bet on horses, you *do* eventually win. The concept of adding to your bet each time you lose assures you of having a big chunk of money on the winner when you do hit the correct horse.

The example was a straight bet, straight amount progression. You're dealing with only a $2 increase with each bet. But there are other ways to follow a progressive plan. If you want to be in line for really big payoffs, you can double the amount of each bet after a loser. That system would look like this:

Race 1	Bet $2.00	Lose
Race 2	Bet $4.00	Lose
Race 3	Bet $8.00	Lose
Race 4	Bet $16.00	Win
Race 5	Bet $2.00	?

You can establish any kind of progression you want and can afford. You may, for example, square the bets and put $16 on the third race, $256 on the fourth race, and so forth.

Any kind of progressive system has certain inherent problems:

> ➤ Although you'll eventually pick a winner, it could be a very long time coming. Everybody who has anything to do with racing has stories about extraordinarily long losing streaks. Great jockeys can lose 100 races in a row (just ask Triple Crown winner Steve Cauthen). Fifty favorites in a row can lose. The Kentucky Derby can be run for 20 straight years with no two-year-old champion ever winning the biggest race for three-year-olds. By the time your losing streak ends, your deficit can look like the national debt.

> ➤ Even if your win comes sooner rather than later, your win will probably be with a horse with fairly short odds. In the Progressive Betting table earlier in this chapter, if your fourth race winner has odds shorter than 3-2, you'll still be in the hole.

Is there a progression that's a little safer and won't require you to bring your betting money to the track in an armored car? Yes. Instead of progressing your bet after one loss, do it after two, three, or four. This way, your total investment at the time of your winning bet may be a little lower, as will be your payoff, but you won't run out of money so quickly.

It's safer and probably more sensible to follow a money management system that calls for bets based on a percentage of your bankroll, rather than specific dollar amounts. Most of these systems work in the opposite manner from progressions.

The Percentage System

Bring a specific amount of money to the racetrack or simulcasting center with which to bet. Choose a percentage to bet on each race. The figure should be no higher than 10 percent if you plan to bet on each race of a 10-race card.

If you've brought $100 and have chosen 10 percent, bet $10 on Race 1. If you lose, bet $9 on Race 2, and so on. When you win, the payoff goes into the bankroll. If you've won Race 2 for a payoff of $30, your bankroll grows to $120, and you bet $12 on Race 3.

You're not going to *tap out* with this system, and you're going to get a chance to enjoy the entire day's race card. Besides, you may walk away with considerably more money than you brought.

From the Horse's Mouth

To **tap out** is to lose the money you set aside for betting.

The Parlay

A percentage system is a kind of parlay because you bet more as you win more, even though the percentage of your bet hasn't increased. To *parlay* means to put your winnings for one race, if any, directly into a bet in the next race.

Some tracks even permit you to make a five- or six-race parlay bet on a single ticket with one visit to the betting window. Here's how it works:

➤ Pick your choices to win in as many races (up to the track's limit for a parlay) as you want to parlay, beginning with the race you feel most confident about. You must make all your decisions in advance of the first race in your parlay, so you can worry only minimally about odds.

➤ Fill out a parlay slip (or remember the race and horses' numbers) and buy the ticket in the amount you want to risk. It can be the track's minimum bet ($1 or $2) if you want to be very conservative.

➤ If your choice in the first race wins, the payoff will go directly into a win bet on the second horse in your parlay, and so on. Just sit back and watch. The computers will figure it all out for you.

You may do your own parlays, of course. Put whatever you win in the first race you bet into the next race, and you've done it. It's less convenient than when you let the track do it for you, but it's worth sacrificing convenience in certain situations:

➤ If the weather is changeable, and you think the track may become wet for a later race.

➤ If you're not sure about track bias, and you want to see its tendencies for the day.

Hedging Your Bets

You can decrease your chances of losing money while increasing your chances of collecting on bets by hedging with place or show wagers. You hedge by:

➤ Betting to win, but betting only a third of what you want to put into the race, and then:

➤ Bet two-thirds to place or...

➤ Bet two-thirds to show on a different horse.

If you have chosen well, you stand a good chance of earning back your investment and a fair chance of making a decent profit.

Betting the same horse to win, place, and show is an *across-the-board* bet. It's the most conservative hedge of all, but it's likely to pay for itself only if the horse in question has pretty long odds.

Dutching

It's theoretically possible to place a bet on every horse in a race and guarantee yourself a profit, no matter which horse wins the race. It used to be done in the days when bookmakers ruled the race betting world.

The system is called *Dutching,* and its concept is simple, although the implementation is neither simple nor cheap. Decades ago, some bettor (or possibly a bookmaker, hoping to protect himself) spent quite a few cold winter nights figuring out a mathematical formula to tell him how much money he should bet on horses at different odds to make sure that the lowest minimum payoff would be more than the total investment in bets. It worked.

He knew that he would, for example, have to bet $12 on a 3-1 shot, $8 on a 5-1 shot, $3 on a 15-1 shot, and so on to make sure that he'd have his profit, regardless of who won. It would still work, if you could buy tickets with set and unchangeable odds. Figure your table, buy your tickets, and wait for your profit.

Unfortunately, the pari-mutuel system sells you the ticket on the horse, not the odds, which change up to post time. Yes, you can wait until the last moment and hope that those odds you see while you're standing at the betting window will be the final ones. But you're more likely to be standing there trying to adjust to last-minute changes and describe 10 different bets with wildly varying totals to the clerk as the machines lock up and you're shut out of the race.

But you can still use some of the Dutching concept to good advantage in your money management betting. Eliminate from your betting equation the horses who have no chance. Even the serious Dutch bettors probably hated to put anything on some of the horses, no matter how strong the guarantee of profit.

Pick three or four most likely winners among those you haven't eliminated. Divide the amount of money you plan to bet on the race among those three or four like so: The horse with the shortest odds gets the most money; the one with the longest odds gets the least. As a rough estimate, put about 25 percent more on a horse with 1 point shorter odds. Here's what your bet might look like on three good horses:

Horse	Odds	Bet
Horse 1	4 to 1	$8.00
Horse 2	3 to 1	$10.00
Horse 3	2 to 1	$12.50

If Horse 3 wins, he'll pay the least, but you'll win more than $36 for an investment of just over $30. If none of the three wins, you're out your $30, but this partial Dutch should work in most cases. There are no guarantees, though.

Chapter 15

The Brave New World of Betting

You don't have to go to the racetrack to place a bet. For a few hundred years now, you've been able to put money on a horse you've never seen, and you don't have to watch one second of the race after you do it. Nowadays, you don't even have to skulk through unmarked doors or whisper into pay phones to do it safely. In fact, many states license and a few operate off-track betting facilities, all in the name of revenue.

Thanks to Alexander Graham Bell, Thomas Edison, Bill Gates, and other techno adventurers, there's now more money bet away from the racetrack than at its pari-mutuel windows. Betting without a trip to the track is a growth industry; it's hugely popular and here to stay. It's usually not the best way to bet on a horse, but it can be done successfully.

Just-the-Facts OTB

Basic off-track betting (OTB) is an old concept. The earliest facilitator of off-track betting was the bookmaker who set up in the neighborhood rather than the grandstand. He's still there, although he and most of his colleagues might refuse your race bets in favor of action on the NFL, the NBA, and the NCAA finals.

Because betting on racing is legal in most states, illegal bookmakers and their customers nowadays prefer to avoid the chance of arrest on something everyone can do legally. But if you like the idea of non-pari-mutuel wagering on horses, there's still one place you can place legal bookmaker-style bets.

Las Vegas and Horses

Live horse racing has failed miserably in Las Vegas, but betting on horses has not. For 50 years, the casinos operated race books featuring odds that they set, just like old-time bookies. You picked your horses, and you waited for the results to be announced. Today, you can still do that for some races, including the Kentucky Derby and the Breeders' Cup.

Several casinos operate future books on big races, and bets placed with these books offer the advantages and disadvantages of all bookmaker betting:

➤ If you're a big bettor, you can wager on credit.

➤ You get to lock in your odds, with no chance of seeing your potential payoff drop along with the odds as race time approaches.

➤ Your odds are locked, but you don't get to opt out if something occurs to your selection, and he doesn't look quite so good going to the post.

Early book betting, particularly the very early kind, can offer the opportunity for huge payoffs to people who are good at assessing a horse's potential for both improving his performance and remaining sound. If you want to place a future book bet on a horse, follow these rules:

➤ Don't bet on any horse with anything that resembles short odds. It's not worth the risk because you can get short odds much closer to race time when it's clear whether they are deserved or not.

➤ Don't bet in the future book on any horse who already appears overraced. If it's February and you're looking at a horse for the Kentucky Derby in May, he'd better not have raced steadily since the previous summer. By May, he will be in his stall, munching hay, and resting up.

➤ Don't bet a horse with a history of unsoundness. Chances are he will be unsound again by race time.

For most races, the majority of Las Vegas race books commingle their pools with those of the racetrack, making a Las Vegas bet like a regular pari-mutuel off-track bet.

OTB Outlets

The simplest OTB outlet includes a betting window or two, a monitor that shows entries and odds, and a loudspeaker to transmit the call of the races. Some of them lack the loudspeakers, and you must look at the monitor to see whether you've won or lost.

OTB outlets provide standard pari-mutuel wagering with your money going into a pool that's either exclusively made up of OTB bets or is commingled with on-track wagering. That can be good or bad:

➤ It's bad because most OTB operators add an extra little takeout, so your payoff for the same odds is less than it would be at the racetrack.

➤ It can be good if the serious, knowledgeable bettors all go to the track. You may get better odds on good horses at an OTB outlet than you do at the racetrack.

OTB outlets are usually more convenient to visit, but what you make up for in convenience is lost in other ways when you take your money to a bare-bones OTB outlet rather than take a trip to the track. You miss:

➤ A look at the horses being saddled and paraded to the start. You don't see who's using up his energy misbehaving or who looks especially healthy and sound.

➤ A look at the racing surface to see its true condition.

➤ A look at the early races on the card to judge the daily track bias.

To make up for the weaknesses of no-picture OTB, you should:

➤ Avoid betting on races where behavior is most likely to play a role, such as two-year-old events.

➤ Avoid races at the beginning of a race meet or early in the year, when many of the horses are coming off a layoff.

➤ Avoid races in inclement weather, because off tracks can be slow, fast, sticky, slippery, or anything in between. You can't judge it unless you can see it.

➤ Avoid a bet until you check the results of the first few races, noting past performances of the winners and placed horses. Try to figure out if the successful horses were early speed animals, if they prefer to stalk the leaders, or if they are in the habit of coming from behind. If you heard the race calls, see whether the successful horses were able to run their typical races and whether the track helped or hindered their preferred racing styles.

Simulcasting

Simulcasting was designed to cure the ills of OTB, and it has proved to be an easy pill to swallow for the racing industry. It emerged in a limited form during the late 1970s and then exploded in the early 1990s as the primary forum for betting on horse racing. Most tracks now enjoy a larger *handle* from off the track than from on, and the percentage of the wagered money they collect in exchange for providing the racing program keeps some of them operating.

From the Horse's Mouth

Handle is the amount of money bet on a race or races.

Simulcast races are transmitted by satellite from the racetrack to other locations where betting is accepted on them. The signals go to OTB outlets, to other racetracks where they're shown between live races, to greyhound tracks, to jai alai frontons, and to other facilities that are permitted to accept pari-mutuel wagering.

Some simulcasting facilities take the word *simulcast* seriously, importing pictures from half a dozen or more racetracks at the same time. Others may show races from only a track or two. Simulcast races allow you to see the horses, judge the track surface, and look at the running of early races, overcoming many of the problems faced by people who have to bet blind at the other OTB parlors. But keep the following in mind:

➤ Some simulcast facilities don't show you pictures of the horses until they're being loaded into the starting gate, far too late to make any betting decisions based on appearance.

➤ Those who show post parade or even paddock pictures can't show every horse all the time. You're more likely to miss a horse acting up than see it.

➤ If signals are being imported from more than one racetrack, you must be very careful to make sure that you're watching the right horse. Horse 4 who's unloading his rider may not be the Horse 4 you're hoping to bet on in the next race.

➤ The betting cutoff at post time is usually extremely strict at simulcast facilities. You may find yourself watching the horses in the paddock but unable to bet on a race because the distant track is running late. Your chance to bet may end at the published post time, not the real start.

➤ Don't use betting systems or money management methods that rely on keeping track of last-minute odds and betting pool changes. That information may not be displayed in time because the monitors are being used for other races.

In-Home Wagering

As soon as they had computer systems that could handle it, most off-track betting enterprises began to offer telephone betting. Customers established accounts, usually through advance deposits, and called in their bets as the mood struck them. Some of the negatives of telephone betting are:

➤ You know even less about the horses than you do at the non-simulcast OTB outlet.

➤ You can't watch odds and pool changes and may often find yourself basing your bet on morning line odds and hoping that they'll hold.

The next step was to link telephone wagering and television broadcasts of races, thereby solving the most serious shortcomings of telephone wagering: the inability to see the horses and the difficulty in determining odds. The technology then moved quickly from telephone/television to interactive television.

Several tracks have begun experiments with equipment that allows bettors to watch races and place bets by pointing a device at the screen. They've been popular, but it's unlikely that either television or racing will want to invest any time soon in the expensive equipment that large-scale interactive systems will require.

Technology invariably explodes on several fronts at once. At the same time that computers became sophisticated enough to handle telephone betting, satellite time became both available and cheap. Racetrack signals could be sent anywhere in the world, and the concept of sending out a signal only locally became old-fashioned almost as soon as it began.

It's easiest to get legislative approval for bets placed by in-state residents on in-state races, but races in another state are another matter; the linking of gambling, the telephone, and television broadcasts potentially runs afoul of several federal laws. Some states and tracks do offer telephone or television betting across state lines, but its legal future is hardly secure.

This rapidly evolving area of gambling is made even more complicated by the technology explosion on a third front: the home computer and the Internet. Hundreds of companies would like to get your betting dollars through your computer, and a couple dozen of them are already in operation. A few more will probably have opened by the time you finish reading this paragraph.

At the moment, most home computer-based wagering is of doubtful legality. The following, however, are almost certainly legal:

➤ An operation in which people in one state bet on races that take place in their own state through a state-regulated system.

➤ An interstate Internet wagering system with the approval of all states involved.

These sites are possibly legal but may not be:

➤ Offshore operations that are run outside the United States but solicit bets from inside the United States.

➤ Operations run from Indian reservations that do the same.

The following is probably not legal:

➤ A U.S.-based, privately run system that solicits bets within the United States, but who knows?

The law, as well as the number of potential betting sites, will change over the next few years (or even the next few minutes). In the meantime, follow these rules if you plan to try and hope to succeed at betting via computer:

➤ Keep track of the law. Some lawmakers want bettors to be prosecuted as vigorously as bet-takers.

➤ If you're convinced it's legal, bet by deposit rather than credit card. Otherwise, you may find yourself losing more than you ever intended or expected.

➤ Unless the law and the betting system provide pre-race pictures of horses and track surface, follow the rules for betting on non-simulcast OTB races.

The Racetrack as Casino

In an inevitable effort to maximize profits, some race-tracks now offer other ways to risk your money. More would do it if their state legislatures would allow them to. Some tracks offer card rooms, others prefer video poker, but most would like to have slot machines, those voracious and mindless revenue generators favored by bettors who'd rather deposit money than think about their bet.

Racetracks, whether they own the slot machines or not, get a percentage of what's bet. They direct this money toward purses, track maintenance, or profits.

When alternative *gaming* was first proposed for racetracks, the traditionalists predicted dire consequences for their beloved sport. Fans, they argued, come to the track with limited funds. Why let it be deposited in machines rather than bet on horses? Supporters argued that it didn't much matter where the money was put, as long as the revenue stream to the track kept flowing.

From the Horse's Mouth

Gambling proponents usually use the word **gaming** to describe non-racetrack wagering. A bet placed under any name is still money risked, and it doesn't seem like a game when you've lost it.

So far, the pro-slots people seem to be winning. Tracks that have installed them have seen less money bet on horses but more money coming into the tracks' coffers. Most of the tracks with slot machines have done well, and some have saved themselves from financial ruin. Financial ruin may still occur at these tracks, but it will happen to the people who deposit their money in the machines.

Most serious horse players stay away from alternative gaming at the track, particularly slot machines, for these reasons:

➤ You can't handicap machines like you can races, and you're trusting your money to chance.

➤ Time spent playing games is time lost for handicapping races.

➤ Money spent on games is money unavailable for betting on horses.

From the Horse's Mouth: The Glossary

Apprentice jockey A rider with less than a year's experience. His mounts get a break in the weights. Because he has an asterisk next to his name in the program, he's also called a bug boy.

Backstretch The long straightaway on the opposite side of the oval from the grandstand. The word also refers to the barn area, sometimes called the backside instead.

Bar shoe A supportive shoe needed by horses with hoof problems.

Barns They're really stables, but around the racetrack you must refer to horse housing as barns.

Bay A horse with a red or brown coat and a black mane and tail. It's the most common color of Thoroughbreds and Standardbreds.

Bias The tendency of every racetrack to favor one style of running over another.

Boots Jockeys wear them, but so do harness horses to protect ankles, knees, and elbows from being cut by their own hooves.

Box When you pick candidates for an exacta or trifecta but aren't sure of the order of finish, you box them. You choose your two or three horses and bet them in every possible order. That's two bets in an exacta and six in a trifecta.

Breakage The few cents on each payoff for a winning bet that's averaged down from the nearest 10 cents. It goes into a special fund to pay off the bettors in minus pools.

Bridge jumper Someone who puts a huge wager on a supposedly sure thing. He bets the horse to show, even though the guaranteed profit is only 5 percent. The bridge figures in if the horse finishes fourth.

Bullet The fastest workout of the day, noted by a bullet sign or asterisk in past performance charts.

Bute The common name for the pain-killing drug phenylbutazone, which is commonly given to American racehorses.

Cannon bone The primary bone between the knee and ankle in the horse.

Catch driver A driver who concentrates on driving, rather than driving horses he trains himself.

Chart caller He makes a simultaneous written record of how individual races are run and how each horse performs.

chestnut A reddish-brown horse. He's likely to be called sorrel if he's a Quarter Horse.

Claiming race A race in which any horse can be bought for a set price. It's the most common kind of race in North America.

Colt A young male horse. Thoroughbreds remain colts until the age of five; Quarter Horses and Standardbreds turn into stallions at four.

Condition books A listing of scheduled races issued by racing secretaries several weeks in advance.

Conformation A horse's physical structure, both overall shape and individual body parts.

Connections Owner, trainer, and other people involved with the horse.

Crossfiring A Standardbred gait flaw that occurs when one hoof strikes the hoof or leg on the opposite corner.

Cushion The amount of loose material, whether sand, dirt, or petrochemical particles, on top of the racing surface. It's usually two to three inches deep on a running track.

Dam A horse calls his mother this.

Dark bay or brown This common color of Thoroughbreds looks black to everyone except the official identifier.

Dark day A day on which no racing is conducted at a particular racetrack.

Dash A single race in which the first place finisher is the winner of the overall event.

Dead Heat When two horses finish in a tie for any of the placings.

Entry If two or more horses owned and/or trained by the same people are entered in the same race, they're called an entry and are considered one horse for betting purposes.

Exacta A bet in which you must pick the first two finishers in exact order.

Exotic wagering Anything other than straight win, place, or show betting.

Figs Not fruit, but figures. These are the results of complex mathematical equations developed by people who think that quantifying speed shown in previous races is the best way to pick winners.

Filly A young female horse. Thoroughbreds are fillies through age four; Quarter Horses and Standardbreds become mares at that age.

Flat Three definitions for the price of one: A Standardbred who doesn't break into a gallop from his trot or pace stays flat. A race that doesn't involve fences is a flat race. A horse who doesn't quite perform up to snuff is flat.

Foal A baby horse. You're most likely to hear it in reference to a stallion's or mare's offspring: Secretariat sired 653 foals.

Furlong One-eighth of a mile. It's the primary unit of race measurement in North America and Britain.

Gallop The horse's fastest gait. It's prized in every racehorse except the Standardbred, who has to be pulled out of contention if he breaks into one.

Game A horse who's brave, determined, or hard-working.

Gaming If you want a more genteel word for gambling, use this one.

Gelding A castrated male horse. Geldings are usually more consistent and better-mannered than stallions, but horses with outstanding breeding are rarely gelded.

Get The offspring of a stallion. Get also refers to a horse's ability to race a certain distance. If he can do it successfully, he can get the distance.

Hand The basic unit of horse measurement, equaling four inches. Horse height is measured from the ground to the high point of the withers, which is the top of the shoulder just in front of the saddle.

Handle The amount of money bet on a race or on a race card. It's more important to racetracks than attendance, because the figure usually includes off-track wagering.

Heat racing To win this kind of Standardbred event, a horse must win two or more individual races before being declared the winner of the event.

Hindquarters What we'd call the hips and buttocks in the human being.

Hock The rear leg equivalent of the knee in four-legged animals.

Hot box A steam room for jockeys. It's not a luxury, it's a necessary device to help them make their assigned weights.

In the money This phrase usually applies to a horse who finishes first, second, or third, providing a payoff to his bettors. Some people consider a horse who earns a portion of the purse to be in the money, so fourth- and sometimes fifth-place finishers may be included.

Jockey's colony This refers to the jockeys who ride regularly at a given racetrack.

Journeyman Once a jockey loses his apprentice allowance, he becomes a journeyman.

Length The body length of a horse. This unit of measurement is used to compare positions of horses at various points in a race.

Lines Harness racing uses this term instead of reins, but it means the same thing.

Maiden special This race is limited to horses who've never won but who have too much potential to risk in claiming races.

Mare An adult female horse.

Morning line The odds set by the track oddsmaker, who attempts to predict how the public will bet.

Off track Any track that isn't fast and dry. It can range from sloppy but very fast to wet, deep, and slow.

Out A start.

Pace This Standardbred gait features legs on the same side moving backward and forward at the same time. Pacers are sometimes called amblers or sidewheelers.

Paint or pinto A horse with splotches of white and solid color. If you see one racing, you're not watching Thoroughbred, Standardbred, or Quarter Horse racing.

Parked When a harness horse is parked, he's still moving, but he has been forced to race wide.

Past performances How the horses performed in their previous races. The charts of past races hold the key to the present race.

Payoff The amount of money you get back on a winning ticket. It's also called the payout.

Pool The total amount of money bet in each wagering category. In the average race, you'll see separate pools for win, place, show, and any exotic bets being offered. A minus pool is one in which there's not enough money to pay back the minimum payoff to every winner.

Post parade This is the first time most of the crowd sees the horses before a race. They walk in front of the grandstand before beginning their warm-ups.

Post position The place in the starting gate for each horse, with the lowest number nearest the rail. They're usually drawn, but they are assigned in some Standardbred races.

Profit The amount of money returned to the winning bettors, minus the money they put into their bets.

Provisional driver In harness racing, a driver who's not fully licensed. It's the equivalent of an apprentice jockey without the weight advantage.

Purse The prize money offered for the race.

Quarter Horse The racing breed that specializes in races of 220 to 660 yards.

Quinella A bet in which you pick the first two horses. If they finish 1-2 in either order, you win.

Race card The entire day's race lineup.

Rating The jockey or driver asks his horse to save energy for a run later in the race.

Rigging A Standardbred's harness, protective equipment, and other gadgets designed to make him perform better, plus the manner in which it's fastened to him.

Ringer A horse who's entered in a race under a name not his own. When it's intentional, it's to make a killing at the betting windows. Nowadays, it's usually accidental and discovered before post time.

Roan A horse whose body is a dark solid color with white hairs intermixed. He'll probably look gray to you.

Route A race that's longer than 1 ⅛ mile.

Scratch The withdrawal of a horse after the entries are announced but before race time.

Shafts The two long pieces that attach the sulky to the horse's harness.

Shipper A horse who travels from where he's trained to race at another track. A shipper is an unknown quantity and often enjoys long odds.

Simulcasting Televised transmission of a race for betting purposes.

Sire A horse's father goes by this name.

Sound Some people use this word to describe only a horse whose legs are healthy and painless. Others consider a horse to be sound only if his legs are strong, his breathing is adequate, and his general health is good.

Spavin A swelling in the rear leg on or near the hock. You're more likely to see it in a Standardbred rather than in a Thoroughbred.

Spot play A race that offers a particularly good bet, such as one with a healthy horse dropping down in class. A sensible bettor usually concentrates his money on spot plays.

Sprint A race shorter than one mile.

Stakes race It also goes by the name of added money race. Horses are either invited by the track or staked to the race by a fee paid by their owners. The fees are added to the purse.

Stallion An adult male horse.

Stamina The endurance needed by a horse who hopes to win any race longer than a sprint.

Standardbred The racing breed that competes under harness, either at the trot or pace.

Stewards The officials who act as judge and jury in the interpretation of the rules of racing, including placements, disqualifications, and suspensions.

Stoopers People who scour the floors after races, looking for mistakenly discarded winning tickets.

Stud fee The amount of money the owner of a mare must pay to have her bred to a stallion. The highest at the moment is about $150,000, enjoyed by half a dozen Kentucky Thoroughbreds.

Sucked along A Standardbred who races directly behind another, benefiting from less wind resistance. If he were a race car, he'd be slipstreaming.

Sulky The vehicle pulled by the Standardbred during a race. He usually trains with a jog cart.

Tack Horse equipment, including bridle, saddle, harness, and miscellaneous accouterments.

Tag A horse who competes in claiming races is running for a tag. The tag is his claiming price.

Taken down A horse who's disqualified is taken down. In reality, it's his number that's taken down. He remains upright.

Takeout The money in each betting pool not returned to the bettors. It goes to the racetrack for operating expenses and to the state for taxes.

Tap out This is what happens when you don't follow the advice in this book and lose all the money you brought to the racetrack.

Thoroughbred The racing breed that specializes in 3/4 mile to two-mile dashes.

Tote board Short for Totalisator board, named for the company that first produced it. This computerized display board tells you what you need to know about odds, payoffs, time, and other details of the race.

Track superintendent He's responsible for maintaining the racing surface. He always plays a role in who wins, and he often has something to do with who survives to race another day.

Train In a broad sense, horses who are being conditioned are being trained. More specifically, to train is to work out at something approaching race speed.

Trifecta Also known as the triple. This bet requires you to pick the first three finishers in exact order.

Triple Crown The most famous Triple Crown is Thoroughbred racing's Kentucky Derby, Preakness, and Belmont Stakes for three-year-olds. If one horse wins all three, he earns the crown. In harness racing, both trotters and pacers have their own Triple Crowns.

Trot The normal midspeed gait of four-legged animals. It features legs on opposite corners moving at the same time.

Turf Grass. It's the most common racing surface in most of the world, but not in North America.

Vet's list A list of horses temporarily prohibited from racing for medical reasons.

Walking ring In flat racing, you first see the horses here, as they're saddled, mounted, and walked around before heading to the racetrack. At some tracks, the horses are saddled in a paddock before proceeding to the walking ring.

Wheel To pick one horse, and then bet every possible combination with that horse in an exotic wager.

Wire The finish line. There's no actual wire involved. It's an imaginary line running between poles.

Yearling A young horse between his first and second birthdays.

Index

M-N-O

Q-R